MY ECUMENICAL JOURNEY

ECUMENICAL EXPERIENCES
AND PERSPECTIVES OF AN
EVANGELICAL CATHOLIC
THEOLOGIAN

CARL E. BRAATEN

ALPB BOOKS
DELHI, NEW YORK

2018 © ALPB Books
All rights reserved in the United States of America

ISBN 1-892921-38-3

American Lutheran Publicity Bureau
PO Box 327
Delhi, NY 13753

Carl E. Braaten, *My Ecumenical Journey: Ecumenical Experiences and Perspectives of an Evangelical Catholic Theologian* (Delhi, NY: ALPB Books, 2018), 139 pp.

CONTENTS

Preface 7

Part One: From Vatican II to the Present

Chapter 1: The Present Theological Situation
   in American Christianity 15
      The New Liberalism in American Theology 17
      Attempts to Reclaim Christian Orthodoxy 21
      Internal Conflicts in Christianity Today 25

Chapter 2: The "Return to Rome" Controversy 29
      Letters in Response to "Return to Rome" 32
      Reunion, Yes, Return, No! 40
      Responses of Four Ecumenical Theologians 42
      Unresolved Issues 47
      Papal and Episcopal Offices of Ministry 50
      A New Type of Ecumenism 55

Chapter 3: The Birth of the Center
   for Catholic and Evangelical Theology 57
      "Call to Faithfulness" Conferences 59
      What is the Center for Catholic
         and Evangelical Theology? 62
      Statement of Purpose 66
      Basic Affirmations 67
      Programs 68
      The Dogmatics Project 69
      The Ecclesiology Seminar 69
      Banquet Address, 2017 71

Part Two: The 500th Anniversary of the Reformation

Chapter 4: We Believe in the One Holy Catholic
 and Apostolic Church 81
  The Birth of the Ecumenical Movement 83
  The Oneness of the Church 87
  The Holiness of the Church 89
  The Church Catholic..90
  The Apostolic Church 91
  Church Unity and Doctrinal Consensus 94

Chapter 5: The Permanent Significance
 of the Reformation for the Church 99
  The Essence of the Reformation:
   Justification through Faith Alone 100
  Worldwide Ecumenical Reception
   of the Doctrine of Justification by Faith 105
  Justification by Faith:
   The Church's Doctrine of Salvation 110

Chapter 6: Anglican-Lutheran Agreement
 on the Gospel 115
  What's to Celebrate? 116
  Is the Reformation Over? 117
  The Evangelical Thrust of the Reformation 118
  Anglican-Lutheran Agreement
   on Justification by Faith 122
  Reception of the Reformation
   beyond Europe and America 123

Chapter 7: Anglican-Lutheran Agreement
 on Full Communion 127
  Anglican-Lutheran Dialogue on the Ministry 128
  Church and Justification Belong Together 131
  Structures of the Emerging Apostolic Church............132
  The Historic Episcopate 135
  Lutherans and Anglicans in Dialogue
   with Roman Catholics 136

To Beryl

My Wife and Tennis Partner

PREFACE

Almost ten years ago I wrote my memoirs as a Lutheran theologian entitled, *Because of Christ*, published by our good friends at Wm. B. Eerdmans Publishing Company. I thought that would be the last book I would write. I sent the manuscript to Bill Eerdmans with the title, "*Propter Christum*," the Latin for "Because of Christ." Every Lutheran theologian with a little bit of learning knows enough Latin to understand what "*Propter Christum*" means. The editors, thankfully wiser than I, nixed my proposed title. Why? A book with a title like that would be impossible to market to their potential readership. Then a few years later I wrote another book, *Essential Lutheranism, Theological Perspectives on Christian Faith and Doctrine*, published by the American Lutheran Publicity Bureau in 2012. I swore to myself and I told my family and friends that it would be my swan song. But alas, it was not to be. Here and now I am writing another book, no doubt my last, about my ecumenical experiences and perspectives as a Lutheran theologian. I will be bringing a perspective which for years I along with others have called "evangelical catholic." I have not told this story before in any detail, and if what I write provides some encouragement to the next generation of Christians committed to the ecumenical goal of achieving Christian reconciliation and inter-communion between separated Christians and Churches, I will count that as a blessing beyond all measure.

Part One will include three chapters which deal with various aspects of my ecumenical journey from the Second Vatican Council to the founding of the Center for Catholic and Evangelical Theology. In the first chapter I will describe the present situation in American Christianity and theology in which ecumenical work occurs, not altogether a happy one as I see it. But that is nothing new. Some are saying we have entered a period of ecumenical winter. However, ecumenical commitment does not depend on the weather. The goal of the ecumenical movement will always be the reunification of the churches for the sake of their universal gospel mission to the nations.

The 500th anniversary of the Reformation was celebrated not only by Lutherans but by Roman Catholics as well as the major Protestant churches that trace their origins to reformers other than Luther, such as John Calvin, Ulrich Zwingli, Thomas Müntzer, Thomas Cranmer, and John Knox. The occasion reminded us that in spite of all of Luther's faults, and they were many, his chief concern was to anchor the church and all its practices in the gospel of Jesus Christ, the precise articulation of which is still most clearly spelled out in the *Augsburg Confession* and the other Lutheran Confessions printed in the *Book of Concord*, authored either by himself or by his friend and collaborator Philip Melanchthon.

Our vision of a renewed ecumenism of the gospel received a major boost when the Roman Catholic Pontifical Council for Promoting Christian Unity and the Lutheran World Federation signed the "Joint Declaration on the Doctrine of Justification," in October, 1999. At the time the good news was reported that they had "consigned to oblivion" the mutual condemnations of the sixteenth century. That would be something special to celebrate, but what makes the *Joint Declaration* more ecumenically transformative is that it has been accepted as a true confession by the World Methodist Council (2006), the World Communion of Reformed Churches (2017), and the Anglican Communion (2017). Lutherans have stated that the doctrine of justification is the "article by which the church stands or falls." Now substantial agreement on the doctrine of justification is shared by five major worldwide Christian communities — Lutheran, Roman Catholic, Anglicans, Methodist, and Reformed. With Lutherans they can now affirm that a major cause of their separation has been removed, giving a green light for further dialogues on still outstanding issues having to do with church, ministry, and the eucharist.

But there are critics. Lutheran critics accuse the *Joint Declaration* of selling out to Roman Catholics, and Catholic critics claim that the statement surrenders too much of the doctrine asserted by the Council of Trent. The differences have to do, first, with the Lutheran understanding of the "*simul*," the belief that even after baptism Christians are simultaneously saints and sinners, and second, with the Lutheran rejection of meritorious good works in salvation. Those are the standard differences of old, so the critics seem to assume that those differences are fixed in stone such that no amount of dialogue seeking mutual understanding could have made a difference.

Reading church history can be depressing. After the Reformation came the religious wars, Catholics and Protestants fighting and killing each other. After the wars subsided the era of competitive missionary evangelization began. Protestant and Catholic missionaries evangelized side by side in the same European colonies in Africa and Asia, but they did not talk to each other; they did not acknowledge each other as sister churches; they were rivals; they engaged in malicious slander and defamation of each other. Then, out of the blue came the first outbreaks of ecumenical dialogue, moving from conversation to collaboration, and even to the brink of consolidation on some mission fields. Past enmities gave way to euphoric dreams of institutional unification of separated church bodies.

Chapter Two of this book deals with an early period in my career as a theologian in which I became at the center of a controversy in which critics accused me of calling for Lutherans to raise the white flag of surrender and capitulate to Rome. The *Christian Century* called this, "The Braaten Brouhaha," but it was actually more like a tempest in a tea pot, started by a misunderstanding and misleading editing brought about by the Lutheran journal, *Una Sancta*.

Institutional ecumenism has fallen on hard times. The World Council of Churches and the National Council of Churches in the USA are no longer regarded as trustworthy agents of ecumenical engagement. This means that ecumenism has had to find other channels. Chapter Three of this book tells about one such attempt, when Robert W. Jenson and I, together with our spouses, Blanche and LaVonne, founded the Center for Catholic and Evangelical Theology in 1992. We believed that the goal of the ecumenical movement is to bring peace and unity in and between the churches that bear Christ's name for the sake of its evangelistic mission to the nations. Jesus prayed not only that "they may all be one," but also that "the world might believe." Church unity and world mission go hand in hand. There may be different models of unity, but they must all have one thing in common, commitment and service to the truth of the gospel. For where unity is not based on truth, it becomes repressive uniformity. The passage in John's Gospel that reports Jesus' prayer that connects unity with belief in him also includes the petition that the love of the Father for the Son may also be in his followers and he in them (1 John 17:26).

Part Two of this book includes four chapters. Chapter Four and Five are nearly verbatim presentations I gave to Lutherans in Charlotte, North Carolina, in commemoration of the 500th anniversary of the Reformation. Chapters Six and Seven are presentations I made to Anglicans in Dallas in June 2017, not only focusing on the Reformation but also celebrating one of the great success stories of the modern ecumenical movement, bringing Anglican and Lutheran Churches into full communion.

We may be approaching the end of the ecumenical era that began a hundred years ago, with much for which to be thankful.

Many things have changed. The religious wars of the seventeenth century witnessed Catholics and Protestants killing each other by the millions. When the wars ceased, Catholics and Protestants continued their confrontation, competition, and conflicts in other ways and on mission fields, not even recognizing each other as true churches of Jesus Christ. The ecumenical movement has made an enormous difference. While the decline of mainline Protestant denominations in Western Europe and America is occurring at a rapid pace, new churches are being born all over the world, especially in Africa and Asia. There may now be more Christians worshipping in China on a Sunday than in the United States. The grace of Christ and the work of the Spirit are wonderfully in evidence in new churches beyond the borders of the declining churches whose missionaries planted them in the nineteenth and twentieth centuries. The living Christ is present within them. But they too are mostly separated from each other. Their answer to Jesus' prayer that "they may all be one" will call for a new burst of ecumenism probably different from what we have experienced. Churches united with Christ will need to find new ways to achieve unity with each other for the sake of the mission of the gospel to the world.

The new ecumenism will need to be inspired by the *agapé*-love of God revealed in Christ. True Christian unity inspired by love will not seek uniformity or conformity. The model of church unity that envisages mergers of existing church organizations may not be what is called for. Unity in love based on the Father's love for the Son, and the Son's love for his church means, in my view, that those who are baptized in the name of the Holy Trinity and believe in Christ as Lord and Savior may be in communion with each other, sharing the same bread and the same cup, yet may not necessarily be members of the same church organization, governed by the same cadre of officeholders. Anyway, there is not an inkling of such an idea in the New Testament and the early church. The political concept of church unity that developed within the context of the Roman Empire attempted to match the power structures of the secular imperium. The global church today is still suffering from and has not repented of the after-effects of such a development.

The modern ecumenical movement has spent most of its time and effort to reconcile the established churches that resulted from the radical schisms of the sixteenth century. Meanwhile, on account of the modern missionary movement millions of new Christians now exist in Africa and Asia with no experience of the organized ecumenical efforts to reconcile and unify the separated churches in Europe and America. The new kind of ecumenism will be less dependent on the planning of experts and officeholders. This new kind of ecumenism is born of the Spirit that moves people to faith, hope, and love. The Spirit blows where and when he wills without checking in at the official headquarters of well established denominations. The new ecumenism born of the Spirit dare not ignore the millions of new Christians created by the missionary outreach of Pentecostalism. This will be an ecumenism not imposed from above but emerging from below at the grassroots, Christians meeting other Christians with hearts filled with the love of Jesus. We cannot be sure of the shape of the new ecumenism born of the Spirit, and even the thought of it may make us feel uncomfortable. But we do know that ecumenism must be born again, renewed by the power of apostolic faith and love, with the gospel of Christ at the center.

PART ONE
FROM VATICAN II TO THE PRESENT

CHAPTER 1

THE PRESENT THEOLOGICAL SITUATION IN AMERICAN CHRISTIANITY

John the Baptist once said he was a voice crying in the wilderness. It is difficult for one writing as a Christian theologian not to feel somewhat the same way in the present situation of Christianity in America and Europe. 2017 was a year marking the quincentennial of the Reformation. Roman Catholics showed good will by joining with Lutherans around the world to celebrate the sixteenth century church reforms proposed by Martin Luther. This was wonderfully amazing in itself, given the fact that the Reformation divided the Western Catholic Church into somewhere between twenty and thirty thousand denominations and sects.

The largest Protestant denominations — Lutheran, Anglican, Presbyterian, Reformed, Methodist, United Church of Christ, and Southern Baptist — are victims of four major trends, perhaps better viewed as tragedies. One, mainline Protestant denominations have drifted far from their founding creeds and confessions; two, they are conflicted by internal divisions and schisms; three, they are all shrinking, losing members by the millions; four, many of their once flourishing theological schools

— those training men and women for the ordained ministry — are closing their doors or barely surviving. To provide the supporting statistics would be needlessly boring.

So, what's there to celebrate when there's obviously so much to lament? Some astute observers have named the present situation as the end of the Reformation[1] or the end of Protestantism.[2] Professor Ephraim Radner, an Anglican theologian, has written a pessimistic obituary of the global church in an ecumenical age, entitled *The End of the Church*.[3] He laments that the churches are in the mess they are because the Holy Spirit has abandoned them on account of their sinful separations. Because the Holy Spirit has taken leave of the churches, so he asserts, the gospel they preach lacks credibility. So again, what's to celebrate? How can we celebrate the disastrous divisions brought about by the Reformation and the membership decline we are witnessing today?

I am writing this book because I believe that in spite of all evidences to the contrary, we do have something perennially great to celebrate. Wherever the Gospel is preached and the Holy Sacraments are celebrated according to the Scriptures, there is the true living church of Jesus Christ. No matter how many or how few there are today who profess to be believers and followers of Jesus Christ and are baptized into the name of the Triune God, Father, Son, and Holy Spirit, they are all members of the one body of Christ. In his Encyclical, *Ut Unum Sint*, Pope John Paul II was absolutely right when he said, "We all belong to Christ." He spoke of churches that were once rivals are now "consigning to oblivion the excommunications of the past." I am writing this book about my ecumenical journey, now over

---

1. Charlotte Hays, "The Beginning of the Reformation's End?" *The Wall Street Journal* (February 26, 2010).

2. Peter J. Leithart, *The End of Protestantism, Pursuing Unity in a Fragmented Church* (Grand Rapids, MI: Brazos Press, 2016).

3. Ephraim Radner, *The End of the Church, A Pneumatology of Church Division in the West* (Grand Rapids, MI: Wm. B. Eerdmans Publishing Company, 1998).

fifty fifty years, because I believe that what the Pope said is most certainly true and well worth celebrating five hundred years after the beginning of Luther's reformation.

The fragmented condition of the churches together with their lack of any coherent doctrinal substance to guide their teachings and practices may account for the apocalyptic obsession with the idea of the end in our time. In addition to the prophetic declarations about *The End of the Church*, *The End of the Reformation*, and *The End of Protestantism*, even more extreme pronouncements have been delivered concerning *The End of Christianity* (James Loftus), *The End of Religion* (Bruxy Cavey), even *The End of God* (Anthony Pinn). These titles have nothing in common with the concept of the end in biblical eschatology. More plausibly they reflect the *fin-de-siècle* mood of their authors.

There is a pervasive sense that the twentieth century world of church and theology we have known has come to an end and that we have witnessed the passing of an era, especially in matters having to do with the ecumenical movement and the centrality of its concern for faith and order. The towering giants who founded and funded the ecumenical movement in the twentieth century are all gone and none have arisen to step into their shoes.

THE NEW LIBERALISM IN AMERICAN THEOLOGY

The present theological situation is characterized by a total collapse of the neo-orthodox consensus in theology that prevailed after World War II. To a large extent this is due to the fact that the over-powering influence of Karl Barth's churchly theology was replaced by the subsequent turn to a plurality of liberal theologies under the aegis of various special interest groups. Latin American liberation theology used the Marxist analysis of society to translate biblical eschatology into revolutionary praxis. The idea of doing theology in a revolutionary situation was later taken over by Black liberation theology, championed by James Cone and Cornell West. Feminist liberation theology is another special interest group, inspired by the writings of Mary Daly, Rosemary R. Ruether, Elizabeth Schlusser Fiorenza, and Sally McFague. Radical theological feminism has had the effect of skewing the ecumenical dialogues because participants were scolded for using the traditional masculine names, symbols, and pronouns for God, including the proper name of the Triune God as "Father, Son, and Holy Spirit." Presumably Jesus cannot be called the Son of God, King, Lord, or Master because such titles of honor connote the biblical patriarchy that reminds us of the continuing oppression of women. A concomitant assault on the doctrine of the Trinity and Christology has been carried even further by the pluralistic theologians of religion. The pluralists are reviving the relativistic theory of nineteenth century liberal theology that all religions worship the same God, only by different names. And, moreover, they all supposedly offer equally valid ways of salvation. The upshot of this way of thinking is that the mission of the church had to be redefined. No longer should it be to invite others to believe the gospel of Christ and plant the church, but rather to join people of good will in supporting human rights and work for a sustainable planet.

The essence of liberal theology is most evident in the way it answers the question that Jesus put to his disciples, "Who do you say that I am?" The stock answer is in direct continuity with the nineteenth century quest of the historical Jesus. Tom Wright calls the current movement "the third quest of the historical Jesus." The quest entails a radical revision of the answer to Jesus' question given by the New Testament and Creeds of the Church. Just as with the Jesus-biographers of the nineteenth century, the sheer variety of portrayals presented by the Jesus-scholars of today is truly astounding. Jesus is depicted as everything from a political revolutionary, a messianic pretender, the founder of a secret society, a Qumran Essene, a Galilean holy man, a wandering Cynic preacher, a Mediterranean Jewish peasant, a counter-cultural charismatic, the founder of an egalitarian community of equals, resulting in hermeneutical and historical scientific bedlam.

The remarkable thing about the new liberalism in theology is that it is now getting major support from American Evangelicals. For a long time Evangelicalism was considered the conservative wing of Protestantism, and it certainly deserves a lot of credit or blame for getting Donald Trump elected president of the United States in 2016, just as they were instrumental in winning the presidency for George Bush in two elections. Evangelicals have given a lot of thought to what it means to be an Evangelical. The movement is a coalition of Protestants who express allegiance either to John Calvin or Jacob Arminius.

Orthodox Calvinists hold to the Five Principles of Reformed Theology, formulated by Dutch theologians at the Synod of Dordt (1618-1619) in the Netherlands, around four hundred years ago. The Five Principles are customarily referred to by the acronym T.U.L.I.P. T stands for Total Depravity. Human beings are by nature through and through sinful, unable to do anything that pleases God. U stands for Unconditional Election. God predestined some for eternal salvation and damned the rest to hell. L stands for Limited Atonement. Jesus died only for the elect, not for all. I stands for Irresistible Grace. God's saving grace is so all-powerful, there is nothing anyone can do to obstruct it. P stands for the Preservation of the Saints. This simply means, "Once saved, forever saved!" The chosen ones are eternally secure.

Jacob Arminius (1560-1609) was a sixteenth century Dutch Protestant theologian who rejected all Five Principles of Calvinism (T.U.L.I.P.). The majority of American Evangelicals are Arminians, and so are the Methodists, following the teachings of John Wesley. Evangelicals in the United States suffer from a split personality — theological schizophrenia. Some are Arminians, some are Calvinists, and they condemn each other's teachings as heresy. This fight does not make the headlines, and the impression is widespread that Evangelicals are one big happy family. That is not the case. They all like Billy Graham, and when he was the uniting force, he kept a lid on the smoldering dispute between the two main types of Protestantism, Calvinism and Arminianism. Lutherans do not have a dog in this fight. The sixteenth Lutheran Confession, *The Formula of Concord*, makes that abundantly clear.

The lack of doctrinal consensus in Evangelicalism has become explicit in the controversy called "Open Theism." Open Theism rejects the classical attributes of God — omnipotence, omniscience, omnipresence, immutability, impassibility, and so on. This is due to the widespread influence of Process philosophy in theological schools, taught principally by followers of Alfred North Whitehead and Charles Hartshorne. Open Theism is also called "Free Will Theism." Does God know the future? Its answer is "No, not until it happens." Does God determine the future? Its answer is "No, not apart from human cooperation." Does God predestine some to be saved and some to be damned. Its answer is "No, not so as to ignore what humans freely decide." Evangelicals are deeply divided on the central doctrines of the Reformation having to do with the way of salvation, *ordo salutis*, particularly on predestination and free will.

Some of the post-conservative Evangelicals are also re-interpreting Jesus' message of the kingdom of God along the lines of the "Social Gospel" of liberal Protestantism. Brian McLaren is a good example of the current Evangelical liberals who believe that the gospel summons Christians to change the world for the better. He is critical of evangelistic preaching that promises individual souls the hope of eternal salvation in heaven as an escape from damnation to hell. He has his eyes on the global challenges that we face here and now in this life. He believes that if the millions of Christians acted out the revolutionary vision of Jesus, they could resolve the crises that civilization faces. He identifies three crises: the "prosperity crisis" brought about by an unsustainable global economy that threatens the planet; the "equity crisis" caused by the growing gap between the rich and the poor; and the "security crisis" that refers to the constant state of war between nations, races, and religions. To support his views McLaren appeals to scholars of the "Jesus Seminar" and their portrayal of a non-eschatological Jesus, thus in line with the "Social Gospel."

In my view it is not only right but imperative to call Christians and churches to the front-lines of action to meet the crises and challenges of our time. That is bare bones Christian discipleship. However, such a vision of the Christian life based on love, peace, and justice may be inspired and motivated by the gospel but it is not the gospel itself. Theologically it is crucial to distinguish between the gospel of the kingdom of God and the ethics of the kingdom, in order to observe the difference between the law of God's justice and the gospel of God's justification of sinners in need of salvation. It would seem that in the view of McLaren and the new liberal evangelical theology, if Jesus' preaching of the kingdom of God cannot be shown to be the solution to the social and economic problems of this world, then his message is irrelevant. To the contrary, for Luther the three great enemies of God and humanity are sin, death, and the devil, not pollution, poverty, and warfare, as challenging as these things certainly are to human flourishing on planet earth. A good share of this book will attempt to make explicit the significance of such distinctions, say, the distinction between justice and justification, law and gospel, earthly welfare and eternal salvation.

ATTEMPTS TO RECLAIM CHRISTIAN ORTHODOXY

The whole story of Christianity and theology in America today must include more than the renascence of old-fashioned liberalism that veers away from the main stream of classical Christianity that the Reformation intended to recoup and that to a large extent was brought up to date (*aggiornamento*) in the Roman Catholic Church at the Second Vatican Council. In fact we are witnessing a vital swing of the pendulum in the opposite direction — toward the reclaiming of Christian orthodoxy east and west. Of course, orthodoxy does not mean the same thing to everyone. One church's orthodoxy may be another church's heresy. That's a debate that belongs on the agenda of the ecumenical dialogues between major Christian traditions. To be as precise as possible, it is customary to combine orthodoxy with a prefix, such as neo-orthodoxy, the common term used to identify the post-liberal theology of Karl Barth and several generations of theologians influenced by his thought. Its strength was the renewal of biblical theology and ecclesial dogmatics, giving rise to creative rethinking the doctrine of the Trinity and Christology.

Radical Orthodoxy is the name of a school of thought introduced into America from England, advocated by John Milbank, Graham Ward, and Catherine Pickstock. It presents a powerful critique of modernity, liberalism and secularism. Radical Orthodoxy reinterprets the history of philosophy and theology to substantiate its key concept of a participatory ontology drawn from Ausgustine in the ancient church, Aquinas in the medieval period, and Jean-Luc Marion in contemporary philosophical theology. For those who love to read philosophical theology in a grand style will discover a treasure trove of ideas in the seminal works of Radical Orthodoxy.

The story of the revival of orthodoxy will also include the contributions of Tom Oden, who coined the term "paleo-orthodoxy" to designate his commitment to mine the wisdom of the ancient church fathers (Patristics), rather than rely on modern academic theologians. His intention was not to write a new theology but to recover the classical theology of the undivided church of the first millennium. The theology of the first one thousand years was produced prior to the Great Schism of 1054 A.D. between Eastern and Western Christianity and prior to the sixteenth century schism between Protestantism and Catholicism. The fruit of Oden's passion for the pre-modern theology of the church fathers is a multi-volume series of "Ancient Christian Commentary on Scripture."

Generous orthodoxy is another term that has found favor among some modern Protestant theologians. It has lost some of its usefulness because many who claim the term for themselves do not agree with each other. The term was coined by Hans Frei of Yale University, an advocate of Karl Barth's theology. Frei used the term to move beyond the liberal-conservative impasse in American theology. The conservatives found Barth's theology too liberal and the liberals found it too conservative. Hans Frei wrote: "Generosity without orthodoxy is nothing, but orthodoxy without generosity is worse than nothing." Frei was aware that American fundamentalism had cast its shadow over orthodoxy, so that in the popular mind an orthodox person is literalistic, anti-intellectual, and bigoted. But Frei was orthodox with a smile and a sense of humor. However, the term "generous orthodoxy" has been co-opted by post-conservative Evangelicals like Brian McLaren, whose theology is orthodox in name only. Some of his fellow Evangelicals use a different label to describe his theology — heresy.

We have identified a number of attempts to reclaim orthodoxy for the church and theology today. Two other movements that contribute to the renascence of orthodoxy in American Christianity are also very much part of the contemporary theological landscape. One has to do with the interpretation of the Bible, the discipline of hermeneutics, and the other with constructing the doctrine of God. Ever since the Enlightenment the interpretation of the Bible has been conducted by using the methods of critical historical science. Scholars have attempted to understand every word and event reported in the Bible against the background of its own time and place. The apparatus of critical historical exegesis used by biblical scholars has become so complicated that the Bible has become a closed book for most preachers and ordinary laity. Currently we are witnessing a remedial backlash. Theologians are reclaiming the Bible as a book of the church. Their aim is to rediscover the ways the Bible was read and interpreted by the church down through the ages. Church doctrine goes hand in hand with biblical exegesis to shape the hermeneutical methods applied. Since the Bible from beginning to end is about the reported acts and words of God, participation in the life and worship of the church provides the best context for interpreting the biblical message today. There is no neutral standpoint from which to read and understand the Bible. In reading the Bible it makes a difference whether one stands within or outside the community of faith. Several new series of biblical commentaries are now being published that apply such principles for the theological interpretation of Scripture.[4]

The second most important theological development has to do with the doctrine of God. The twentieth century renewal of the Christian doctrine of the Triune God is the best example of ecumenical orthodoxy. Karl Barth and Karl Rahner, a Reformed Protestant and a Roman Catholic, were both instrumental in writing a new chapter in the history of trinitarian theology. Both of them lamented that the doctrine of the Trinity has become dysfunctional in Christian theology and church practice. The doctrine of the Trinity was virtually discarded in nineteenth century Protestant theology, except for the few influenced by the philosophy of G. F. W. Hegel.[5] Immanuel Kant expressed the common opinion: "From the doctrine of the Trinity, taken literally, nothing whatsoever can be gained for practical purposes."[6] Friedrich Schleiermacher placed his treatment of the Trinity in the Appendix of his dogmatics. Roman Catholic, Eastern Orthodox, and Protestant theologians are finding common

---

4. The two publishing Houses are Wm. B. Eerdmans Publishing Company and Brazos Press.

5. Examples are Isaac Dorner and J. C. K. von Hofmann.

6. Quoted by Jürgen Moltmann, *The Trinity and the Kingdom*, p. 6.

ground in their understanding of God.[7] It is to be hoped that this profound ecumenical consensus will move the churches forward to concelebrate their communion in Christ and to cooperate in their witness to the gospel.

INTERNAL CONFLICTS IN CHRISTIANITY TODAY

Intense conflicts have developed within the mainline Protestant denominations — Episcopalian, Presbyterian, Reformed, Methodist, Lutheran, and United Church of Christ. The one word that best describes the present situation is "polarization." The churches are divided between conservative and liberal wings, between traditionalists and progressives, reflecting the great divide between red states and blue states. The Teacher in the Book of *Ecclesiastes* says, "There is nothing new under the sun" (Eccl. 1:9). Church historians would confirm that. The Apostle Paul addressed the conflicts in the churches he founded. He wrote, "Now I appeal to you, brothers and sisters, by the name of our Lord Jesus Christ, that all of you be in agreement and that there be no divisions among you, but that you be united in the same mind and the same purpose" (1 Cor. 1:10).

There were bitter quarrels in the early church between the Gnostic, Jewish, and Pauline Christians. Gnostic Christianity never died out. It was forced to go underground. Today it is

---

7. Here is a partial list of theologians who have contributed to the renewal of Trinitarian theology, in addition to Karl Barth and Karl Rahner: 1) Eberhard Jüngel (a Lutheran), *God as the Mystery of the World*; 2) Wolfhart Pannenberg (a Lutheran), *Systematic Theology*, 3 vols.; 3) Jürgen Moltmann (Reformed), *The Trinity and the Kingdom*; 4) John Zizioulas (Greek Orthodox), *Being as Communion*; 5) Walter Kasper (Roman Catholic), *The God of Jesus Christ*; 6) Catherine LaCugna (Roman Catholic), *God For Us: The Trinity and the Christian Faith*; 7) Miroslav Volf (Pentecostal), *After Our Likeness. The Church as the Image of the Trinity*; 8) Colin Gunton (Congregational), *The Promise of Trinitarian Theology*; 9) Robert W. Jenson (Lutheran), *The Triune Identity*; 10) Leonardo Boff (Roman Catholic), *Trinity and Society*.

finding a hospitable home in American religion. The essence of Gnosticism, old and new, is that God and the soul are one. To find God one only needs to enter into the depths of one's own self. No external word is necessary, neither the message of the Bible nor the preaching of the gospel. Gnostics believe that religion is a private matter. A person has no need to attend a church and worship with an assembly of fellow believers. The decline of membership in the mainline churches has been rapid and steep. Attendance at worship has been dropping steadily. The mainline churches are getting older and grayer. They are losing the younger generations.

The internal conflicts in the mainline Protestant denominations are driving them to the brink of schism. Here is a statement from a Report of the Concerned Clergy and Laity of the Episcopal Church: "Today, there are two religions in the Episcopal Church. One remains faithful to the biblical truth and received teachings of the Church, while the other rejects them.... Radical activists seek to replace biblical truth and Godly morality with secular humanism and moral relativism. We have become a church which contradicts its own teaching."[8] Conservatives and liberals read the same Bible but they derive vastly different conclusions about what it says and means.

There are at least five hot-button issues that trouble the mainline churches. 1) One that touches every person attending worship services is the naming of God. For traditionalists the proper name of God is "Father, Son, and Holy Spirit." God's name is holy and unalterable. For revisionists the name of the Holy Trinity is an arbitrary combination of metaphors that can be changed to suit contemporary sensibilities. 2) A second issue has to do with the uniqueness of Jesus Christ. Is Jesus Christ the one and only Savior of the world or are there many savior figures offering equally valid ways of salvation? Are there many roads that lead to God, as many as there are religions? Revision-

---

8. http://www.episcopalian.org

ists and traditionalists do not agree on the right answer to this question. (3) The third issue has to do with the authority of the Bible and the challenge of historical relativism. Does Scripture still function as the definitive norm for all Christian doctrine and morals? (4) Related to the issue of biblical authority is the role of the church and its creeds in providing normative guidelines of interpretation. By what authority should Christians today claim that one interpretation of the Bible is to be accepted rather than another? The church is not a democracy in which the majority decides what is doctrinally true and ethically right. (5) Finally, no one can doubt that there is widespread conflict over matters of sexual morality. The nub of the issue in current debate is whether the churches should bless same-gender unions and ordain pastors and bishops married to partners of the same sex.

Roman Catholics in the United States are also polarized, deeply divided over the meaning of the Second Vatican Council. Progressives are pushing for greater reforms. They believe that Pope Francis is a welcome ally in their cause. Traditionalists are trying to turn back the clock to undo the reforms they believe have gone too far to accommodate contemporary culture. An extreme group of conservative theologians and bishops have even filed a law suit accusing Pope Francis of heresy and aim to have him deposed. Progressives call for the empowerment of the laity, ordination of women, and voluntary celibacy for priests. Traditionalists pull in the opposite direction, in spite of the fact that priestly celibacy is being called into question by the shameful scandal of sexual abuse of children by priests. Progressives believe that the requirement of celibacy is a root cause of sexual deviancy. The legal settlements on behalf of victims has cost the Roman Catholic Church billions of dollars, and the laity are ashamed and angry. I have a Catholic friend who told me that his way of protesting is to place just one penny in the offering plate when he goes to mass.

The main focus of the book I am writing concerns the ecumenical movement and its mission to reconcile the divided churches in order to achieve full visible church unity, in short, to fulfill Jesus' prayer that "they may all be one." We have provided a brief description of the present situation in American Christianity and theology because that is the context in which the next ecumenical endeavors will necessarily take place. Realistically, the ecumenical movement has lost momentum on account of the divisions and controversies within the churches that we have discussed. At times the traditional differences between the churches may seem quite trivial compared to the apostasies and heresies rampant within them. Some lay folks shop around for a congregation to join that suits them. Others simply vote with their feet, walk away never to return. Still others believe it is their calling to stay where they are, fight the good fight and finish the race, no matter what.

Yet, there is reason for hope. Many pastors and priests remain at their posts, faithful in ministering to the Word and the Sacraments. Many congregations are busy reaching out to the unchurched with the gospel and serve their communities as good Samaritans. It is our prayer that God in the power of his creative Spirit will channel all our passions to the advancement of his kingdom "on earth as it is in heaven." It is our prayer that God will reconcile the churches so that their divisions will no longer be impediments to their mission to go and tell the saving gospel of Jesus Christ to all who do not yet believe in his name.

CHAPTER 2

THE "RETURN TO ROME" CONTROVERSY

I became an ecumenical theologian during the Second Vatican Council (1962-1965). Toward the end of the Council I gave an ecumenical address at a pastoral conference of the Northern Illinois Synod of the Lutheran Church in America, at the request of its Bishop, the Rev. Robert Marshall. He asked me to offer an assessment of Vatican II from a Lutheran theological perspective. I accepted the invitation even though I was not adequately prepared to do what he asked. My ecumenical experiences were limited. As a graduate student at Harvard Divinity School in the 1950s I was exposed to an ecumenically diverse faculty. In his autobiography Paul Tillich asserted that he was a Lutheran by conviction. He had just arrived from Union Theological Seminary in New York to teach systematic theology at Harvard, and that was the main reason I chose to attend Harvard rather than Yale or Chicago Divinity Schools. Krister Stendahl was a Swedish Lutheran professor teaching New Testament, who later became dean of the faculty. John Dillenberger was a United Church of Christ professor teaching Reformation History. Paul Lehmann was a Presbyterian teaching Christian theology and ethics. Richard Reinhold Niebuhr was a United Church of Christ professor teaching Modern Theology.

Father Georges Florovsky was an internationally famous Russian Orthodox theologian teaching Patristics (Church Fathers). Milton V. Anastos was a Greek Orthodox theologian teaching Eastern Christianity, noted for proving (*sic*) that "Nestorius was Orthodox." Harry Austryn Wolfson was a Jewish historian who wrote seminal works on such famous Jewish philosophers as Philo, Maimonides, Averroes, and Spinoza, and surprisingly also on the Church Fathers. Ralph Lazzaro was a Unitarian linguist, teaching the biblical and classical languages to graduate students. Conrad Wright and George H. Williams were Unitarians, teaching Church History. George Buttrick was a Presbyterian Professor of Homiletics. A more ecumenically diverse faculty of theology would be hard to find, but little to no attention was given to the modern ecumenical movement and the worldwide quest for Christian unity among major churches and denominations. Ecumenism never quite made it anywhere as a theological subject worthy of serious scholarly attention.

A few years laters I had a taste of ecumenical dialogue between Lutherans and Catholics when as an instructor at Luther Seminary in 1960 I was asked to join a group of students and professors to travel to St. John's Abbey in Collegeville, Minnesota, to discuss theology with its monks and teachers. Father Godfrey Diekmann was the leader of the Catholics and Professor Warren Quanbeck was our leader. Father Diekmann was a leading liturgical theologian who served as one of the American *periti* at the Second Vatican Council. For several days we exchanged views on the usual controversial topics that Catholics and Lutherans had contentiously debated for centuries — faith and works, law and gospel, justification and sanctification, simul *iustus et peccator*, the Pope and Mary, and to no one's surprise we did not learn much and neither did they. But we did experience something liturgically unforgettable, namely, praying and worshipping together with the monks of St. John's Abbey. That taught us that theological dialogues from faith to faith flourish better when conducted within the setting of common prayer and worship. I know there are Lutherans who don't believe in praying with

Christians other than themselves. Happily, we were not of their ilk. The Benedictines at St. John's Abbey had much to teach us about liturgical worship. I took away from this experience the sense that worshipping together may express our unity in Christ better than anxious striving for consensus in doctrine.

With this limited background in matters ecumenical I wrote my address word for word and delivered it with all the gusto at my command. It was printed in *The Record* of the Lutheran School of Theology, Maywood Campus, under the title, "The Tragedy of the Reformation and the Return to Catholicity."[9] *The Record* was the in-house magazine of the seminary, read mostly by its alumni. The article would not have become newsworthy except for the fact that the editor of *Una Sancta,* the Rev. Richard John Neuhaus, thought otherwise. Richard Neuhaus asked for permission to publish an edited version of my article in *Una Sancta*, which turned out to be a drastic abridgment of the original, omitting many paragraphs that would have given a more balanced view of what I said and meant. Neuhaus had the gift of seeking and gaining wide publicity for projects he deemed worthy of such. He contacted the editor of the *Religious News Service,* and within a week headlines were appearing in local newspapers across the United States, "'Return to Rome' Urged by Lutheran Theologian." This despite what I wrote in the original version printed in *The Record*. These are my actual words: "If evangelical catholics harbor hope of reunion with Roman Catholics, they certainly do not and cannot mean *return* to the Roman Catholic Church as Roman. The concept of 'return' is inadequate simply because it suggests that the Protestant party is the prodigal wanderer who comes home, while the Roman Church is the waiting Father. There has been prodigality on both sides, and the Roman side has not been standing still. Furthermore, the concept of 'return' which grates upon Protestant

---

9. Carl E. Braaten, "The Tragedy of the Reformation and the Return to Catholicity," *The Record*, Lutheran School of Theology, (August, 1965), Vol. 70, No. 3, 5-15.

nerves does not reflect Pope John's admission that responsibility is divided, and there is equal blame on both sides. The idea of a mutual advance converging upon the future fulfillment of what is valid on both sides is a better working hypothesis. It does not require either side to deny its own history, but through further historical development, it allows for future reconciliation."[10]

The editor of *Una Sancta*, Richard John Neuhaus, chose to delete the paragraph that made clear that I did not propose that Protestants "return to Rome" as though they could accept it as their new church home. But the cat was out of the bag, and once something appears in the news, many people are gullible enough to believe it must be true. This experience taught me never to believe the headlines or news reports until they are carefully fact checked, not even when they break in my favor.

LETTERS IN RESPONSE TO "RETURN TO ROME"

The response to the "return to Rome" headlines was fast and furious. I started receiving letters from concerned clergy and laity from virtually every denomination and state, and a few from overseas. The idea of Protestants and Catholics reuniting in one visible church of Jesus Christ struck a nerve. Catholic responses tended to rejoice that finally a Protestant theologian had the good sense to accept Rome's standing invitation to Protestants to "come home." Protestant responses were mostly outraged by the preposterous suggestion that heirs of the Reformation should return to the very Roman Church still in bondage to the doctrinal heresies and superstitious practices Luther sought to expunge. Here are some quotations from the angry letters that show — even after the transformative changes the Council effected to bring the Roman Catholic Church up to date

---

10. "The Tragedy of the Reformation and the Return to Catholicity," *op. cit.*, 13-14.

(*aggiornamento*) — the deep-seated anti-Catholicism that transfixed the mind and soul of American Protestantism.

Written by a confirmed Lutheran woman in Milwaukee: "You have shocked me. Do you mean to say that what Martin Luther did was all in vain? If you want to be a part of Rome, that is your decision. But don't take anyone with you. How would you like to sit with beads and pray to Mother Mary? She comes before Christ in the Catholic religion. Heaven forbid that we should obey the Pope, who tells us when to eat meat or fish."

From an unsigned letter: "Dear Mr. Naive!: I hope your Lutheran Church gives you to the Pope. It is a sad commentary on the Lutheran Church that you are a member. There is no freedom in the Catholic Church. If you wish to make slaves of your children and grand children, at least leave other people alone. Go be a priest, you'll see what you gave up. No priest can marry, so you would have no children (that you could acknowledge). In France the priests live with their housekeepers, and no one cares. In Quebec loose living is the thing, since no divorce is sanctioned. A Catholic herself told me so. H. G. Wells claims that the giant octopus of the Catholic Church has brought poverty and made the people grasp at the straws of Communism. You want to drag all of us back into the Dark Ages. God forbid!"

Written by a Missouri Synod Lutheran woman: "I never cease to be amazed about people like you speaking for others without mentioning their names. Please don't speak for me. Please contact the nearest Missouri Synod Lutheran pastor and hear what he has to say about what the Reformation meant. I am opposed to the ecumenical movement and intellects like you within the church."

Another unsigned letter, this one from Cadillac, Michigan: "Why should Protestant Christians want to return to Roman Catholicism which is the most powerful, widespread and subtle of all unbiblical religious movements? Roman Catholicism is a false religion and is leading millions to perdition. I don't see how any born again person can advocate we return to Rome."

Written by a Lutheran in Bethlehem, Pennsylvania: "If you want to return, all well and good, but in this city where the Roman Monopoly holds sway since the Bethlehem Steel Company imported many Europeans in the early days of its operation, there are many of them who have joined the Lutheran Church, glad to be free from the slave tactics of the Roman Hierarchy. There is no thought in this city of anyone returning to Rome. I think the president of your Synod should give you a passport out of your church, and then you will be free to join the Romans. Here's a salute to Luther who made it possible for so many to escape the yoke of the Catholic Church."

Written by a proud Lutheran woman in DuBois, Pennsylvania: "I am both surprised and disgusted with such theological teaching as yours. Martin Luther, of whom I am a descendent, thought it was necessary to reform and separate. I am a teacher of an adult Lutheran Women Bible Class whose children have married Catholics through ignorance of doctrines. You speak for yourself only and not for the great Lutheran Church for which my father and grandfather worked so hard. My grandfather studied Latin, Greek, and Hebrew, knew the original doctrines, and couldn't be wrong. The Catholic Church is trying to take us over in a world government. Don't be a dupe. When Lutherans join Catholics, I'll seek another church. Either get sincere about our great heritage or get out of the ministry."

From an unsigned letter mailed from New Haven, Connecticut: "We like sauerbraten but we do not like the statement in the newspapers coming from you. Being a member of the Missouri Synod Lutheran Church, God forbid that we should want to return to a Roman home. What has happened in Rome the past two years shows that the greatest theologian, Martin Luther, was centuries ahead of his time. The Roman Catholic Church, with its *hocus pocus* commercialized faith and awe-inspiring pageantry, is not a religion, but a huge Frankenstein political group operating in the guise of religion and riding high and handsome in the name of God, with a machine that rides rough shod over non-Catholics who do not bow before their power. Catholicism is no different than Communism; both want to rule the world by hook or by crook. We never see anything spiritual in connection with the Roman Catholic Church, what with all the bingo, carnivals, fairs, raffles, chances on autos, etc., etc., anything to squeeze the last dollar out of its members and the public at large. Return to Rome? NEVER! We want to remain Americans in every sense of the word."

From an unsigned letter using scatological language: "The ecumenical church of which you speak is not a church at all. You and your ilk are trying to establish a 'Hell Hole' comprised of Religious Queers and Communist Conspirators under atheistic control to eliminate the Christian Church and Christ's teaching completely. Whom do you think you are fooling? I was reared in a Lutheran home and I think you are mentally unbalanced and repulsively queer. No one in his right mind would make the statements you made. Hurrah! Hurrah! For the 'Devil's Little Helper' and the Communist Big Shot — spelled with an 'i'."

From a Lutheran woman in Milwaukee: "Your view of reunion with Rome is a great disservice to all Protestants, to all Christians and especially to all Lutherans. The Catholic Church has certainly not made any worthy reforms. Catholics still believe in and worship the Pope as God. Catholics pray to Mary and all the Saints and trust in them. Catholics pay money to their Church for prayers for forgiveness or to redeem someone from Purgatory, or they perform good deeds to gain salvation. Let us not consider unity on earth with any group that so openly preaches a faith that is against the words of our Lord. God, the one just judge, will complete the unity of true Christians in Heaven."

From a retired Lutheran pastor in Minneapolis: "It would seem that a person advocating a 'return to Rome' has very little knowledge of the history of the Reformation. I have lived neighbor to and been friends with Roman Catholics, but how can a Lutheran clergyman fall in love with Roman Catholic doctrine? The stand that you are taking borders on treason to the faith you confessed at your ordination, you being a teacher at a Lutheran School of Theology, the financial support of which comes from the constituency of the Lutheran Church. To every sound Lutheran this appears preposterous. If the Roman Catholic Church is so precious to you, it seems you should follow John Henry Newman's example by taking the first step to join your favorite Church, rather than get your bread and butter from the Lutheran Church. I was a student at your seminary more than 50 years ago, but I am glad not to be there with professors of your kind."

From a letter sent from Fullerton, California: "Don't believe in phantasy and fairy tales. There are 4000 Communist clergy plants in the National Council of Churches. Are you one of them?"

From a distraught Lutheran in Brazil: "I was only a Junior at Luther Seminary in St. Paul when you taught there but I did not have the occasion to be in any of your classes. When I read your statement that Protestantism should return to the Roman Catholic Church in our daily newspaper, my first reaction was one of anger, then of frustration thinking to myself: If he could only see Latin American Catholicism as we see it in Brazil, he wouldn't think that way. But as I continued to reflect on your statement, I concluded that you must know that. You are an intelligent person and have seen the world and know what is going on, so your problem is not narrowness or bigotry. It must be something else. Your theological perspective is being formed and informed by a childish rebellion — perhaps your parents' faith or perhaps some overly strict pastor in your childhood. Your total motivation seems to be to get attention at any cost — like a child that beats his head on the floor. My psychology professor suggested one time that the best cure for a child doing this is to shock him with a bucket of cold water. This is precisely what you need, to bring you back to some basic facts of life. You were not ordained to serve your emotions but the Lord. Stop crying like a child and acting like a delinquent in adult wrappings. The church has been shocked enough — thanks to men like yourself. Enough! I must go back to work now and try to explain why we are here if our Lutheran Church thinks the Roman Catholic Church is O.K. now."

Not all letters were of that kind. Here are several responses from well-meaning sympathetic Catholics.

From a devout Catholic woman in Cloquet, Minnesota: "Martin Luther was a German. I am a German. My father was born in Germany and came to America. He married a Lutheran girl. She turned Catholic because my father was a Catholic. She had the Catholic religion explained to her before converting. Her two sisters also turned Catholic. History tells us that one day Luther's mother came to him and asked her son, 'Tell me the truth. Should I become a Lutheran or stay a Catholic'? Martin answered his mother, 'Lutheran is easier living, but Catholic is better dying.' She said to him, 'I will always remain a Catholic.' Martin Luther was forced to give up his Catholic religion by threats from the rulers of Germany until his death. This was in the 1500s. God wants us all to belong to the church that he himself started. He said, 'On this rock I will build my church.' If you can get Lutherans to turn to the Catholic religion, you will be a big Saint one day. Please turn Catholic and get others to do that."

A letter from a Catholic woman in Evanston, Illinois: "I have been a close observer of the World Council of Churches, having attended its sessions here in Evanston. I want you to know how joyful I am at what you are saying. It is indeed heartening. About ten years ago I was converted to the Roman Catholic Church, and ever since I have been wondering what is the psychology that keeps Protestants from entering onto and walking along the superhighway that Jesus established as he appointed Peter: 'And upon this rock I will build my church.' He didn't say 'churches.' An increasing number of Protestants will out of necessity come to realize that Jesus established the Papal system. The Holy Spirit invisibly moves within it. The unauthorized alternative is the system in which various and sundry people claim personal direction from the Holy Spirit. The result is a 'do it yourself' religion that has produced 250 or more Protestant divisions — a despair in Heaven and a problem on earth. Protestantism is a convenient endless spiritual smorgasbord from which one can take as much or as little as one chooses."

A letter from a Roman Catholic priest in Rochester, New York: "You seem to be a scholar willing to view facts objectively with courage to present them in the face of almost certain criticism from your confreres. Let us then face the facts. 1) The Catholic Church is and always has been the mainstream of Christianity, roughly two-thirds of the world's Christians; 2) Luther's was a personal problem of despairing of being able to avoid sin. According to his theory we are all cesspools of sin, born in sin, living in sin, and dying in sin. His criticism of the church was directed against the traditional theology of the church rather than against certain abuses in the church at that time. Luther would then have broken with the church even if there had been no abuses. 3) The Lutheran reformation was essentially no different than any of the heresies of the ancient church — Arianism, Nestorianism, Manicheanism, and the rest. Heresy means changing the traditional Christian doctrine handed down to us in all parts of the world and in every century. The church may never teach anything new. To do this an infallible church is necessary. Man-made churches always die like other human institutions. I feel that if I can present these facts to further the truth, I shall be well rewarded for my efforts and may even hope to receive some reward hereafter."

The following opinions are from a Catholic priest sympathetic to Luther: "While attending Loyola College in Baltimore, I got into some rather heated arguments about Martin Luther. It was then, and still is, my contention that Martin Luther's original break was not intended to be a break at all. The historians of that era have given us accounts that are not accurate. I believe that many reforms were due at the time of Luther, but because of circumstances and limited communications, Luther was made a 'scape-goat.' I feel that Luther received a raw deal. I have often wondered what the result would have been if we had a Pope like John XXIII in Luther's day. I am remembering you in every Mass I am privileged to say."

A letter from a life-long Lutheran woman in St. Paul with an interesting perspective: "I agree completely with your statement regarding Luther's original objective, and I feel that the Lutheran Church of today would disappoint, perhaps dismay him. Could we not become the Catholic Evangelical Church? I suggested several months ago that all present Lutheran bodies merge under that name, and then acknowledge Luther's influence by adding: 'Sponsor of all Lutheran Institutions, Orphanages, Schools, Hospitals, Nursing and Retirement Homes.' Returning to the control of the Roman Church could broaden us in some respects but narrow us in others. Should we not protect and retain sound thinking that has advanced knowledge and freedom in Lutheran countries?"

A letter from a Lutheran priest in the Church of Sweden: "With a very great enthusiasm I have read your article. Its main ideas correspond exactly to my own views of our situation in relation to Rome. I have already translated your article into Swedish and I would like to have your permission to publish it in a Swedish magazine. I must confess that I disagree with one of your points. You call the Roman dogma of papal infallibility a 'heresy' and you use the same epithet to the modern Marian dogma. Is it necessary to use such harsh language in this connection? I do agree that the dogmas were and are quite unnecessary and hurtful to the work of reunion. But are they untrue, even a heresy? Personally I dare not state such an opinion against the successor of Peter and the world episcopate of the Roman Catholic Church. Do you not think that we will be able to find a way of integrating them in an Evangelical Catholic connection without expressly denying them? I would be very glad if you would kindly answer this question and allow me to publish the answer as well."

REUNION, YES, RETURN, NO!

Having read these and many other letters, I found it necessary to do what I could to clarify my views, based on the article printed in *The Record* and explain why the abridged version in *Una Sancta* was misleading. Richard J. Neuhaus, the editor of *Una Sancta*, wanted to continue the discussion in the following issue of *Una Sancta*.

The most surprising intervention in this whole episode was an editorial in *The Christian Century*, entitled "Protestant Hara-kiri." The editor, Kyle Haselden, responded to my article, "Rome, Reformation, and Reunion," printed in *Una Sancta* virtually in the same way as those angry Protestants, Lutherans among them, whose letters I quoted at length above. He assumed that my article was calling for Protestants to return home to Rome, a proposal he dubbed "absurd" and "mischievous" and "odious" and "dangerous." In a letter I wrote to the editor I reminded him that nowhere was I pleading for Protestants to return to Rome and that moreover leading Roman Catholic ecumenists had long since abandoned the "return to Rome" theme in speculating on a possible future reunion of divided churches. Not once did I use the word "return." Instead I wrote about reunion, reconciliation, and reunification of Protestants with Roman Catholics. I wrote of longing to be integrated with Catholic Christians in the "one, holy, catholic, and apostolic church" confessed by all churches that subscribe the Nicene Creed. I suggested to the editor that every time I used the word "catholic," he took it to mean "Roman." Also, that the most plausible explanation for falsifying what I wrote is that he never read my article but based his biased opinions on the misleading headlines that appeared in the local newspapers.

My article used a parable which likened Protestants to exiles. This was not an original idea of mine. The metaphor of "exile" was used by the leading Lutheran ecumenist, George Lindbeck, in an article entitled, "The Ecclesiology of the Roman Catholic Church."[11] He wrote, "The Protestant exiles have become thoroughly acclimatized in their new ecclesiastical homes... The Catholic Church was for the early Protestants the one and only church, it was their home church, it was their ecclesiastical homeland — but it was under enemy occupation. The government had become tyrannical. It drove out not only those who would reform it, but even those who asked for nothing more than the freedom to preach the gospel. There was nothing to do except to form a government, an ecclesiastical order, in exile. But the Reformers at first no more thought of this as a new, a second church than De Gaulle thought of his war-time regime as a replacement, a substitute for France."[12]

The reference to De Gaulle took me back to my days in Madagascar when the Island was under the jurisdiction of the Vichy government, serving as the puppet of Hitler's occupation army. Thus I began my address with a parable, based on a bit of World War II history. In June of 1940 Hitler's army invaded and conquered France. Marshal Pétain became the head of the state under Hitler. However, many a loyal and patriotic Frenchman protested against Marshal Pétain and the Vichy government which he headed. A man volunteered to lead an army of French volunteers to liberate their fatherland — General Charles de Gaulle. Frenchmen became divided. The majority remained in France, loyal to the Vichy government of Pétain. In Britain De Gaulle rallied the freedom fighters in exile for the purpose of liberating their homeland and be reunited with their fellow countrymen. The free French protesters did not forget the reason for their exile. They had no intention of becoming accustomed to life outside of France, to turn their temporary arrangement into a permanent situation. What if they forgot the reason for

---

11. George Lindbeck, "The Ecclesiology of the Roman Catholic Church," *Journal of Ecumenical Studies*, Vol. 1, No. 2, 1964.
12. George Lindbeck, *op. cit.*, 246.

their exile and instead settled down in some other country, with no thought of every going back? If that would have happened, we would have good reason to call it a tragedy — something akin to the tragedy of the Reformation.

The free French under de Gaulle never imagined they could return to France as long as a false government was in control of their homeland. As the exiles saw it, a radical change would have to take place. As exiles they remained French from head to foot. They were aware that the institutions they had to improvise were provisional and their interim status would become obsolete once the goal of liberation and reconciliation was attained.

The thrust of the parable is clear. The heirs of the sixteenth century Reformation are "Catholics in exile." The crisis situation in which they are living, no matter how long, is abnormal, and they must keep hope alive that it is temporary. One purpose of the Reformers' protesting movement was to keep the goal in sight of reuniting with all those who belong together, all who believe in Christ and are baptized into his living body — the *una sancta catholica et apostolica*. We know beyond a shadow of doubt that Luther never intended to emigrate out of the Church in which he was baptized, confirmed, and ordained, in whose churches he preached and in whose school of theology he taught. He said in effect, "If you are a Christian, please don't identify yourself by my name." Well, we have done it anyway ever since and no doubt will continue to do so with no apology, albeit with a renewed self-understanding as evangelical catholics in the Lutheran stream of the Christian tradition.

RESPONSES OF FOUR ECUMENICAL THEOLOGIANS

Editor Richard J. Neuhaus invited four leading ecumenical theologians to contribute an essay to a symposium dealing with my article, "Rome, Reformation, and Reunion." They were:

Albert C. Outler, Methodist, Professor of Theology at Perkins School of Theology, Dallas, TX

Warren A. Quanbeck, Lutheran, Professor of Systematic Theology at Luther Theological Seminary, St. Paul, MN

George A. Lindbeck, Lutheran, Professor of Historical Theology at Yale University, New Haven, CT

Robert McAfee Brown, Presbyterian, Professor of Religion, Stanford University, CA

I was very pleased not only with the support I received from such high-ranking theologians, all very experienced in ecumenical dialogue with Roman Catholics, but also with their severe castigation of the erroneous editorializing of *The Christian Century*. Albert Outler, with whom at a much later date I was privileged to debate the differences between Wesleyanism and Lutheranism on the doctrine of justification, with particular focus on the phrase, *simul isutus et peccator* — the idea that a Christian is at the same time righteous and sinner, righteous on account of Christ and yet sinful by nature. Some pundit once said, in baptism the Old Adam is supposed to have drowned, but he sure can still swim. I argued what for me was the obvious point that if a Christian were not still sinful after baptism, what would be the point of asking daily for the forgiveness of sins? Does any Christian ever reach the point of no longer needing to ask the good Lord for forgiveness? The Wesleyan doctrine of sinless perfectionism says "Yes," whereas every confessional Lutheran would insist, "Never!" I do not remember Outler's rejoinder, except that he did not accept my understanding of what Wesley had in mind by "sinless perfection." When a statement of fact or doctrine is not believable on its face, theologians not seldom are wont to say, "Don't take it literally."

The topic of the symposium was about the relations between Catholics and Protestants after the Council and the news reports that a Lutheran theologian in Chicago calls for Protestants to return to Rome, their ecclesiastical homeland. After a careful reading of what was printed in both *The Record* and *Una Sancta*, Outler stated bluntly, "Reunion by return — the *Century*'s pet peeve — is expressly ruled out.... Nowhere is there a whiff of reunion by repudiation." And, "What Braaten does stress — and one had thought this was now a commonplace among ecumenists — is that the prospect of reunion by convergence is both more hopeful and more immediate than we were able to imagine a decade ago.... What the *Century*'s reaction has made uncertain is whether the questions Braaten raised can even be debated in an atmosphere calm and non-defensive to avoid old dead-ends of partisan polemics."

Warren Quanbeck, once my New Testament professor when I was a student at Luther Seminary in St. Paul, also confirmed that my address to the Lutheran clergy did not regard a "return to Rome" as an appropriate or desirable way of achieving church unity. At the same time Quanbeck thought that my parable of the Free French in exile was open to misunderstanding. For the Free French led by De Gaulle do intend to "return to France." This is true, but the return of the exiles is subject to the precondition of a radical change of government in the homeland. Quanbeck does understand the intent of the parable is to point to the provisional character of the Reformation and its intention to assert true catholicity and to reform the Church. This underscores the well known fact that Luther was a loyal son of the Church and never intended to be schismatic. After Luther was excommunicated, church unity was fractured. Thereafter any hope of reunion would be contingent on restoring traditional catholic doctrine and practice against certain late medieval innovations, under the primal authority of the Word of God. Quanbeck concludes his essay by asserting: "The reports that Professor Braaten advocates a 'return to Rome' not only misrepresent his concern and understanding of the problem but also undercut Roman Catholic ecumenists who, in the spirit of the Second Vatican Council and of Pope Paul's encyclical *Ecclesiam*

Suam, strive to bring about genuine ecumenical activity within the Roman Catholic Church."[13]

George A. Lindbeck was Professor Emeritus of Historical Theology at Yale University. He passed away January 7, 2018. He was a good friend for many years and served as a member of our Board of Directors of the Center for Catholic and Evangelical Theology. We will always remember him as the most important Lutheran ecumenical theologian of the twentieth century. We had several things in common, apart from church and theology. We were both missionary kids, he from China and I from Madagascar, and we both loved to play tennis. Along with Professor Edmund Schlink of Heidelberg University he was an official observer representing the Lutheran World Federation at the Second Vatican Council. He also made the most important contributions to the drafting of the documents of the Lutheran-Roman Catholic dialogues. Lindbeck began his essay, "Reunion for Mission," with these words, "Why the furor? Why object as strongly as some have done to Carl Braaten's 'Rome, Reformation and Reunion'? Why misrepresent him? Substantially the same points have been made by others besides Braaten without arousing much excitement. Every reputable historian insists that the Lutheran reformers did not intend to found a 'new church' and desired nothing more than a renewal of the whole of Christendom which would make possible the disappearance of their own emergency ecclesiastical orders. Surely those who question the continued viability of this attitude are — prima facie, at least — more open to the charge of betraying the Reformation than is Braaten.... I myself have said (or intended to say) everything Professor Braaten has, and practically no one took exception.... What Braaten is saying is that Protestantism should make unmistakably clear that it is not interested in the indefinite continuance of its independently organized existence, and it is willing to make all kinds of structural 'sacrifices' for the

---

13. Warren A. Quanbeck, "The Path of Dialogue," *Una Sancta*, Volume 23, Number 3, 20.

sake of the fuller actualization of the Church catholic, which is also the Church renewed."[14]

Robert McAfee Brown is the fourth symposiast, a well known Protestant theologian whom I did not personally know but who had acquired a well deserved international reputation as an articulate ecumenical theologian. He began his essay saying that after reading all the documentation regarding my article — pros and cons — "I am forced to the conclusion that he has been the victim of an unusually bad press."[15] At that time no one had used the phrase "fake news," but it would have been applicable. He went on to say, "Braaten's original article in *Una Sancta* seems to me a sober, reasoned and balanced appraisal of what we must do today about the Protestant Reformation, worthy of more responsible treatment than that accorded it.... I had better make clear what I understand Professor Braaten to have said. The concern of the reformers was never to establish an independent church, but to reform the existing Church. Nevertheless a tragic division developed, for which both sides are to blame. But an even greater tragedy is that the division has come to be accepted, especially by Protestants, as normal. In this situation, what is needed is not a continued polarizing of the two sides, but an 'evangelical catholicity' on both sides that will combine both continuity and reformation. The situation of the Protestants is analogous to the situation of a government in exile, save that the latter always wishes to be restored to its homeland, whereas Protestants seem content to remain where they are.... What is called for is what Professor Braaten describes (in disavowing 'return') as a 'mutual advance converging upon the future fulfillment of what is valid on both sides'.... Thus it would seem that Professor Braaten's article is a significant next step in the ecumenical dialogue.... Protestants and Roman Catholics live

---

14. George A. Lindbeck, "Reunion for Mission," *Una Sancta*, Volume 23, Number 3, 21-24.

15. Robert McAfee Brown, "A Significant Next Step," *Una Sancta*, Volume 23, Number 3, 23.

in a new era in which we are both discovering that the terrain that separates us ... is for the first time rich with promise, and with the hope of a redeeming harvest."[16]

I responded to the four symposiasts gratefully acknowledging that they understood what I intended to communicate in my article, especially for taking pains to correct the many distortions in the news reports. I entitled my response, "Reunion, Yes; Return, No." The release of the Religious News Service (RNS) on which many of the news reports in the public media were based stated that I was "urging Church union on the basis of a Protestant 'return to Rome'" and that I was calling upon my "fellow Protestants to look upon the Reformation as an event in history which, having accomplished the reforms it set out to bring about, must now become past history. The 'exiles' of that period, he maintained, should now return to their 'ecclesiastical homeland' — the Roman Catholic Church."[17] That is very far from what I had in mind. In fact, I stated that there was still a lot of unfinished business that had to be taken up and resolved after the Second Vatican Council in inter-confessional dialogues between Roman Catholics and Protestants of all denominations, with Lutherans rightfully in the vanguard of that agenda. For the past fifty years Lutherans and Catholics have been engaged in dialogues that have taken up all the controversial matters of doctrine and church practice that have traditionally divided our two churches.

UNRESOLVED ISSUES

The Protestant critics of my article thought I was overly enthusiastic about the ecumenical progress and the hope of ecclesial reunion brought about by the Second Vatican Council, whereas

---

16. Robert McAfee Brown, "A Significant Next Step," *Una Sancta*, Volume 23, Number 3, 23-26.
17. Carl E. Braaten, "Reunion, Yes; Return, No," *Una Sancta*, Volume 23, Number 3, 27-33.

in fact I raised a number of questions that remained unresolved after the Council. I pointed out that many of the differences between the churches of the Reformation and the Roman Catholic Church identified by the sixteenth century Council of Trent and the nineteenth century First Vatican Council remained unresolved by the Second Vatican Council. They would need to be taken up by the post-conciliar dialogues and they were. Heading the list is the dogma of papal infallibility, making assent to it a requirement of salvation. My article bluntly labeled the dogma a "heresy," much to the chagrin of the Swedish Lutheran priest referred to above. Next in line is the escalation of Mariology in modern Roman Catholic doctrine and piety, which Protestants regard as a serious heretical innovation, widening the gap between Rome and the Reformation. Both were affirmed at the highest level of authority *ex cathedra*, pronouncements of the Pope considered infallible. My Anglican friend, Geoffrey Wainwright, professor emeritus of theology at Duke Divinity School, once quipped that the Pope has spoken *ex cathedra* only twice and he was wrong both times. Both Papal infallibility and the modern Marian dogmas have been thoroughly addressed by Lutherans and Catholics in Dialogue, USA.[18]

The Roman Catholic Church entered modernity with fear and trembling. It published the *Syllabus of Errors*, a list of eighty propositions condemned as erroneous by Pope Pius IX in 1864. Leading up to Vatican II it went through a period of retrenchment, circling the wagons, turning in on itself. The in-breeding resulted in a loss of catholicity, becoming more Roman than Catholic. My article made the bold claim that the Roman

---

18. *Papal Primacy and the Universal Church*, Lutherans and Catholics in Dialogue V, edited by Paul C. Empie and T. Austin Murphy (Minneapolis, MN: Augsburg Publishing House, 1974).
Teaching Authority & Infallibility in the Church, Lutherans and Catholics in Dialogue VI, edited by Paul C. Empie, T. Austin Murphy, and Joseph A. Burgess (Minneapolis, MN: Augsburg Publishing House, 1978).
The One Mediator, The Saints, and Mary, Lutherans and Catholics in Dialogue VIII, edited by H. George Anderson, J. Francis Stafford, and Joseph A. Burgess (Minneapolis, MN: Augsburg Publishing House, 1992).

Catholic Church had subverted the meaning of catholicity by equating it with Roman. Our common Creed does not say we believe in the one, holy, Roman Church. What kind of category is "Roman?" Is "Roman" synonymous with "Catholic"? Lutherans are still asking these questions. When Edmund Schlink wrote his reflections on the Second Vatican Council, he always referred to the Roman Church, not the Roman Catholic Church.[19]

I also stated in my lecture that the Roman Catholic Church refused to acknowledge other churches as truly and authentically church. The Council referred to non-Roman churches as "ecclesial communities," and stated that only the Roman Catholic Church "subsists in" the one, holy catholic, and apostolic Church." For me that is a mistake, and calls into question the integrity of the ecumenical movement, for if the ensuing dialogues are not between equals, they are one-sided, at least, lop-sided. One party has *prima facie* the upper-hand, poised to assume the role of senior partner, teaching others what they need to possess to share in the fulness of the church. It should be gratefully acknowledged that the best Roman Catholic theologians could not be accused of treating their Protestant and Orthodox counterparts as inferior or lesser than equal partners in dialogue. The problem is inherent in the dogma, not with the theologians or the Council itself. What is needed to give hope to future ecumenical work is a new self-understanding of the Roman Catholic Church, one which sets aside a superiority attitude that assumes it is at the center of the universe of churches.

Within a year my mind was moving on to embrace the new eschatological theology of hope coming out of Germany, spearheaded by Wolfhart Pannenberg and Jürgen Moltmann. In 1967-1968 I was in England, having been awarded a Guggenheim Scholarship for a year of research and writing at the University of Oxford. I chose to take my sabbatical in Oxford because my friend, Robert W. Jenson, was there, serving as dean

---

19. Edmund Schlink, *Ecumenical and Confessional Writings*, Volume 1, edited by Matthew L Becker (Vandenhoek & Ruprecht, 2017).

and tutor of Lutheran students at Mansfield College. By chance or providence Jenson's mind had taken the same turn as mine, toward reaping the fruits of the new affirmation of the futurist dimension in biblical eschatology. I was writing my book entitled, *The Future of God, The Revolutionary Dynamics of Hope* and Jenson was writing his book, *The Knowledge of Things Hoped For, The Sense of Theological Discourse*. Our Oxford conversations resulted in a book we co-authored, *The Futurist Option*.

PAPAL AND EPISCOPAL OFFICES OF MINISTRY

After I left Oxford to return to Chicago, I became preoccupied with other theological concerns,[20] although my commitment to ecumenical matters continued to be expressed in terms of giving

---

20. I have described the various theological concerns other than ecumenism that preoccupied my time and energy in my theological memoirs, *Because of Christ*. After all, I was trained to be a teacher of dogmatics; I was not an experienced ecumenical expert. Robert W. Jenson and I co-edited two volumes of *Christian Dogmatics*, still in print 35 years later. I became interested in radical politics, during the misbegotten war in Vietnam, and published my book *Christ and Counter-Christ, Apocalyptic Themes in Theology and Culture*. My wife, LaVonne, became interested in health and nutrition and founded and managed a number of health food stores in Chicago, and we co-authored a book, *The Living Temple, Theology of the Body and Foods of the Earth*. I received the Franklin Clark Fry Award in 1974 which financially supported a worldwide tour in Asia, Africa, and South America, lecturing at schools and seminaries founded by nineteenth century missionaries, Lutheran, Methodist, Presbyterian, etc. The climax of this experience resulted in the publication of *The Flaming Center, A Theology of the Christian Mission*. Lutheran unity in America took center stage in the early 1980's. There was no prospect that the Lutheran Church–Missouri Synod would join the ALC and the LCA in the movement for Lutheran unity in America. I organized a church-wide conference held at the Lutheran School of Theology at Chicago, inviting the most important Lutheran theologians to debate the theological issues facing American Lutheranism. I edited the proceedings of this conference entitled, *The New Church Debate*, Fortress Press, 1983. Some were calling for the merged church to be so new that no one would be able to recognize it. One pundit opined – "And that's what happened."

lectures in various venues — mostly in Catholic and Protestant seminaries and pastoral conferences around the country. It was generally acknowledged that the ecumenical train was stalling, perhaps even grinding to a stop. Some observers were saying ecumenism is dead. Especially young people seemed uninspired by institutional ecumenism managed by church bureaucracies that produce statements no one reads and that make no difference. Dreams of the coming great church were dashed on the rocks of realism, giving way to lethargic acceptance of a sectarian future and the bad old days of schism after schism.

Many were saying at the time that we were heading into an ecumenical winter, facing chilly relations between and within churches and denominations. I did not want my commitment to ecumenism to fluctuate with the weather. In 1967 I published an article, "The Reunited Church of the Future,"[21] in which I tried to tackle the structural problem of the church, which continues to be the major hurdle on the way to the reunion of the churches. The question is whether there is any biblical justification for a hierarchical model of church order essential to being the Church of Jesus Christ. My answer provided the following provisos. 1) The way that church offices are structured is not essential to the gospel. 2) Nonetheless, a future reunification of separated churches will include papal and episcopal offices of ministry that became well established in ancient Christendom. 3) Papal and episcopal offices will be acceptable to Protestants, and certainly to Lutherans, once they have been divested of every authoritarian feature, both in theory and practice. I believed then, and I do now, that these assertions comport well with the Lutheran *Formula of Concord*.

Something more needs to be said about church order from a confessional Lutheran perspective. A reunited church of the future will not subordinate the truth of the gospel to the unity of the church. That would only bring about a new rupture as severe as the Reformation schism. Christian faith seeks unity

---

21. Carl E. Braaten, "The Reunited Church of the Future," *Journal of Ecumenical Studies*, no. 4 (1967), 612-28.

in the truth of Christ and refuses to be indiscriminately joined with any system of belief indifferent to the question of truth. Church unity must be based on unity in the gospel. A visible continuity in church structure is no sufficient compensation for lack of unity in the gospel of Christ. This is the non-negotiable concern of any Lutheran church or theologian true to the core beliefs of the sixteenth century Lutheran Confessions.

The reality is that many Lutherans today still believe it was appropriate for the first generation of Lutherans to be rid of the traditional church structures, such as the threefold office of ministry, bishop, pastor, and deacon, as well as the papal office of universal supervision. This attitude belies the fact that this happened against the will of the Lutheran Reformers. Melanchthon wrote in the *Apology of the Augsburg Confession,* Article XIV on "Ecclesiastical Order," that "We want at this point to declare our willingness to keep the ecclesiastical order and canonical polity, provided that the bishops stop raging against our churches. This willingness will be our defense, both before God and all the nations, present and future, against the charge that we have undermined the authority of the bishops." I affirmed this teaching by stating that it is quite unimaginable that the reunited church of the future would evolve new structures minus the papal and episcopal office. These structures serve as representative signs of the continuity of the Church of Jesus Christ and the Apostles through the discontinuities of time and history. The Church of Christ does not reinvent itself in every new generation. The apostolicity of the Church is safeguarded by a number of vehicles, in addition to the ecclesiastical offices, such as the canonical Scriptures, The Creeds of the Church, and the rites of liturgy, working together to transmit the tradition of the gospel to every new generation of the people of God.

In my next ecumenical experience I was privileged to share several days with Professor Wolfhart Pannenberg and Father Avery Dulles at John Carroll University. The three of us were invited to speak at a conference sponsored by the 1969 Walter and Mary Tuohy Chair Lectureship.[22] The main theme was the development of dogma in an age of historical consciousness. Pannenberg speculated on the shape of a new Christian unity emerging in our time, without the requirement of uniformity. Dulles reflected on the theme of modernization (*aggiornamento*) that was a driving concern of Vatican II, to assist the Church to address the deepest concerns of people today. Once Catholics and Lutherans reach substantial agreement on the doctrine of justification, the article by which the church stands or falls, which I believed was possible if not inevitable, the chief remaining stumbling block between Lutherans and Roman Catholics was bound to be the Petrine office, and particularly the accompanying dogma of papal infallibility. I followed up the points I made in my article, "The Reunited Church of the Future," eager to find out how my thoughts on episcopacy and papacy would be received by a predominantly Catholic audience. I reasserted that the reunited church of the future would be equipped with structures that are recognizably continuous with both papal and episcopal offices. I was brash enough to assert that if Protestants, including Lutherans, can accept the Canon, Creeds, and Liturgies of the ancient church, there is no good reason why they (we) cannot accept the offices of the early church created to cope with her needs on her missionary journey. I say, there is no good reason, but I know that this is a hard pill to swallow for Protestants, harder than is the doctrine of justification by faith for Roman Catholics. At the same time I stated that these offices will pave the way for a new union of Christian Churches only on the precondition that they sacrifice every authoritarian feature in theory and practice. I believed at the time, perhaps too optimistically, that the impetus of the Council's commitment to *aggiornamento* — modernization, bringing the Church up to-date — would convince the Roman

---

22. *Spirit, Faith, and Church*, by Wolfhart Pannenberg, Avery Dulles, S. J., and Carl E. Braaten (Philadelphia: Westminster Press, 1970). The German translation of this book was strangely entitled, *Kirche Ohne Konfessionen? Sechs Aspekte ihrer künftige Gestalt*, with a Foreword by Professor Heinrich Fries (München: Claudius Verlag, 1971).

Catholic Church to abandon its heritage of heteronomous authority, inimical to the gospel of freedom — "the freedom for which Christ set us free."[23] The sociological reality is that among the rank and file of Roman Catholics there is a widespread revolt against the Grand Inquisitor model of church authority carried over from the Counter-Reformation. The Episcopal and Petrine offices may be legitimated in an evangelical and catholic church as instruments of unity and servants of apostolic faith and doctrine. Every church in every generation needs the offices of ministry that remind us that as believers in Christ we are to be together, to do things together, that in our common baptism we are united with Christ, and therefore also have a shared memory that reaches back to the Apostles and strains forward in anticipation of an eschatological future when God will sum up all things in Christ.

One effect of my "Tragedy of the Reformation" lecture and article was that it received an unanticipated positive reception from Roman Catholic theologians and church leaders, leading to numerous invitations to speak at Roman Catholic conferences, seminaries, and colleges. As a result I came into contact with and gained many new conversation partners, a veritable "who's who" among Catholic theologians — Hans Küng, Eduard Schillebeeckx, Johannes B. Metz, Avery Dulles, George Weigel, Michael Novak, David Tracy, Gary Anderson, Carl J. Peter, George H. Tavard, Bernard Lonergan, Matthew Lamb, David Burrell, Francis Schussler Fiorenza, Kilian McDonnell, Susan K. Wood, Margaret O'Gara, Paul Griffiths, Russell Hittinger, William T. Cavanaugh, James Buckley, Brian Daley, Roger Haight, John Dominic Crossan. This list does not include my Lutheran friends who joined the Roman Catholic Church — something I myself have never seriously considered doing — nevertheless, the fact that this was happening kept me focused on the importance of Lutheran-Catholic relations.[24]

---

23. Galatians 5:1.
24. They were Richard J. Neuhaus, Robert L. Wilken, Reinhard Hütter, Mickey Mattox, Leonard R. Klein, Bruce Marshall, Michael Root.

A NEW TYPE OF ECUMENISM

In 1970 I was invited to participate in a new type of ecumenical congress, which was promoted as a paradigm for the future. The conference was held in Florida and based on the thought of the Jesuit theologian, Father Bernard Lonergan. The conference was called "Ongoing Collaboration." The purpose was not only to study and respond to Lonergan's philosophical theology, but to initiate a process in which intellectual power is applied to illuminate a wide range of issues facing Christianity and humankind. Those invited to the congress were intellectual leaders in their fields and broadly representative of various types of Christian theology. Among them were: Elizabeth Anscombe, Michael Novak, Langdon Gilkey, Thomas J. J. Altizer, Leslie Dewart, Charles Davis, Senator Eugene McCarthy, James M. Robinson, Schubert Ogden, Walter Ong, and John McKenzie. When I received the invitation to attend, I wondered, "Who is Bernard Lonergan?" I never heard his name during my graduate studies in philosophy and theology, a sad commentary on the parochial nature of graduate education in the best Divinity Schools, preoccupied as they were mainly with modern Protestant theology.

Bernhard Lonergan taught at Gregorian University in Rome (1953-1966), producing dogmatic writings on the Trinity and Christology. At 65 he retired and took up residency at Regis College, Toronto, and from there his well deserved fame began to spread in the United States. He published a massive volume entitled, *Insight: A Study of Human Understanding* (London: Longmans, Green & Co., 1957). This was followed by his *Method in Theology*, which took into account new challenges from existentialism and phenomenology. For his Catholic students Lonergan was building a bridge from the outdated world of Thomistic scholasticism to post-Kantian critical philosophy and philosophy of history (Wilhelm Dilthey).

After Vatican II one began to hear of Lonergan's name through a widening circle of students who had studied at the Gregorianum in Rome. Lonergan's fate was similar to that of every great theologian or philosopher, in giving rise to right-wingers and left-wingers. Conservatives hailed Lonergan as a new Aquinas, providing new foundations for the ancient Christian dogmas. Liberals tended to see Lonergan as a new Kant, whose significance is not in providing a system of truths but in showing how to think, not so much a position to hold as a way to go. The ecumenical influence of Lonergan's thought will be gradual and long-lasting, because it will help theologians in dialogue to discuss issues on their merit and out of the pure desire to know the truth of the matter, and not act as servile partisans of any church's bureaucratic propaganda. The real purpose of theology in dialogue should be to advance insight and to attack what Lonergan calls *scotoma* — blind spots that result from limited understanding. A credible ecumenism will require churches and theologians seeking reconciliation and reunification to collaborate to overcome biasses, prejudices, and partial viewpoints inherited from the era of religious conflict and church division, in which each sectarian party or sect is hellbent on seeking its own advantage.

CHAPTER 3

THE BIRTH OF THE CENTER FOR CATHOLIC AND EVANGELICAL THEOLOGY

In the autumn of 1961 I arrived in Maywood, Illinois, with my family to teach at the Lutheran School of Theology. I had accepted a one year position as visiting professor, with no assurance it would be extended. The school had a search committee to find a successor to Professor George Forell, who resigned suddenly to accept a position as Professor of Theology at the University of Iowa. I was assured that I would be considered as his replacement, but with no guarantee. I took my chances. I had served for three years as pastor of the Lutheran Church of the Messiah in North Minneapolis. That was a wonderful experience that proved to be invaluable preparation for teaching seminarians, most of whom were studying to become Lutheran pastors. If one is to teach what pastors need to know, it helps to have been a pastor oneself. But I was eager to move forward with my teaching career for which I had spent seven years of graduate studies beyond college — University of Paris, Luther Seminary, Harvard Divinity School, and Heidelberg University. In the spring of 1962 the faculty voted to recommend me for the position of professor of systematic theology.

Thirty years later in the spring of 1991 I resigned from the Lutheran School of Theology at Chicago. I was fed up with the teaching conditions that prevailed at the seminary at that time. The majority of students were unprepared to undertake the study of theology in a serious way. The academic prerequisites for admission to the seminary had been gradually reduced to the point where anyone with a college degree was acceptable. Traditionally the college curriculum for a pre-seminarian would include the classical languages, Greek and Latin, the history of philosophy, courses in Old and New Testament, history of Christianity, and possibly world religions. In my graduating class from Luther Seminary in 1955 at least seven went on to study for doctorates in theology from Princeton, Yale, Harvard, and Chicago. Very few graduates from the Lutheran School of Theology at Chicago were prepared to go on to study for doctorates in theology. That's bad enough, but worse is that the seminary requirements for ordination had been so dumbed down that few were theologically qualified to become Lutheran pastors. That was my firm conviction, so I offered my resignation with no clear idea of what to do next.

The first thing I did was to call my good friend, Robert Jenson, who was teaching at St. Olaf College, my *alma mater*. When I told him I had resigned and why, he knew what I was talking about because he had had a similar experience and had reached the same conclusion teaching at the Lutheran Theological Seminary in Gettysburg. After many lengthy phone conversations, including our spouses as well, we decided we would found a theological center with an ecumenical mission. And that's what we did in 1992, in Northfield, Minnesota. In my mind I was not turning to ecumenism because I was giving up on Lutheranism. The opposite is true. I became deeply involved in a movement to call the Evangelical Lutheran Church in America (ELCA) to be faithful to its reformational origins and its confessional Lutheran identity.

"CALL TO FAITHFULNESS" CONFERENCES

Within a few years after the merger of three Lutheran churches — the American Lutheran Church (ALC), the Lutheran Church in America (LCA), and the Association of Evangelical Lutheran Churches (AELC) — to constitute the ELCA, many Lutheran pastors, theologians, and lay folks were voicing protests against trends that would eventually make the ELCA just another liberal Protestant denomination. Convinced that this would be ecumenically disastrous, I invited the editors of three Lutheran journals to a meeting at my house in Chicago to plan a conference that would sound an alarm that the whole church would hear and hopefully heed. We called the conference, "Call to Faithfulness," which was held at St. Olaf College, June, 1990. One thousand pastors and lay leaders attended, a sign that a nerve had been struck.

Robert W. Jenson gave the keynote address, addressing the question, "What would it mean for the church to be faithful?" He observed that many were attending this conference because they feared that the faithfulness of Lutheranism in America had become doubtful, in that "gnosticism is triumphing within it." He asked, "To whom or to what are we to be faithful?" His answer was: "To the particularity of the God of the Bible, the God of the Exodus, narrated in the Old Testament, and the God who raised Jesus from the dead, proclaimed by the apostles. The root of the Christian doctrine of the Trinity is grounded in the biblical story of the God who saves and whose proper name is Father, Son, and Holy Spirit. The attempt to exchange the Triune name of God for some other triadic metaphors is a tell tale sign that gnosticism had reared its head. One of Jenson's memorable statements has often been quoted, "A church ashamed of God's name is ashamed of her God." Jenson went on to expound the essence of faithfulness — to the church's mission to bring the message of the gospel to the nations and ages, to the apostolic telling of the gospel, and he went on to speak of faithfulness to the canon, creed, and confession of the church as norms of her life and ministry. Jenson's address was followed by presentations by other well known Lutheran theologians. Gerhard Forde, James Kittleson, Joseph Burgess represented *Lutheran Quarterly*, Richard Neuhaus and George Lindbeck represented *Lutheran Forum*, Robert Jenson, Paul Sponheim and I represented *Dialog*. Any well informed reader of these journals would know very well that these theologians disagreed among themselves on many things, especially on the interpretation of Luther's theology, the present-day meaning of the Reformation, the authority of the Ancient Creeds and the Lutheran Confessions, the significance of the ecumenical dialogues, involving Lutherans and Roman Catholics and other Protestant denominations. So what did these representatives of different types of Lutheranism in America have in common, to bring them together in the "Call to Faithfulness" conference at St. Olaf College? They could agree that their differences are real but not church-dividing, not rising to the level of heresy or apostasy. They felt that they shared responsibility to address the threats that face American Lutheranism in our time. They feared that their church was accommodating the ideologies that threaten to compromise the gospel and the Christian faith. History will judge whether their fears were well founded.

A second "Call to Faithfulness" conference was held two years later, June 9-11, at St. Olaf College. Some reporters alleged that they had heard a lot of "Higgins Road"[25] bashing at the first conference. That is true and it continued at the second conference. And yours truly was one of the guilty parties. The message of the two "Call to Faithfulness" conferences was that we are in a struggle for the soul of Lutheranism. The ELCA was being taken hostage by a system of beliefs and practices incompatible with the Christian faith. In a desperate attempt to attract consumers with a product whose appeal is success, not faithfulness, self-esteem, not discipleship, techniques, not

---

25. Referring to the headquarters of the ELCA.

truth, the ELCA was joining the parade of Liberal Protestant pluralism and reductionism.

Speakers at the conference named the trends that were contending against fidelity to the Gospel normed by the canonical Scriptures, the Creeds of the Church, and the Confessions of classical Lutheranism. The ELCA had made a big deal about recovering the Office of Bishop in its Full Communion agreement with the Episcopal Church USA, but regarding discipline in matters of church doctrine it didn't amount to a hill of beans. Article 28 of the *Augsburg Confession* confesses this truth: "According to divine right, therefore, it is the office of the bishop to preach the Gospel, forgive sins, judge doctrine and condemn doctrine that is contrary to the Gospel, and exclude from the Christian community the ungodly whose wicked conduct is manifest. All this is to be done not by human power but by God's Word alone. On this account parish ministers and churches are bound to be obedient to the bishops according to the saying of Christ in Luke 10:16, 'He who hears you hears me.' On the other hand, if they teach, introduce, or institute anything contrary to the Gospel, we have God's command not to be obedient in such cases, for Christ says in Matt. 7:15, 'Beware of false prophets.'"

At these conferences we named the demons, but we failed to exorcize them. Life in the ELCA continued to go downhill after the conferences. Radical theological feminism insults the name of the Trinity, Father, Son, and Holy Spirit. The theology of religious pluralism avers that there are many roads that lead to God, denying the uniqueness of Jesus Christ and the Gospel of salvation in his name. The ideology of historical relativism asserts that there are no absolute authorities, undermining the authority of Holy Scripture. American cultural religion, aka neo-gnosticism, is a new form of the ancient heresy that believes that God encounters us not through the "external Word" (*verbum externum*), but is accessible in our souls if we go deep enough through transcendental meditation. The cult of egalitarianism attacks the fundamental institution of the holy ministry. Ordained ministers of the church have no more authority than their janitors. Having lost the sense of a divinely instituted authority, the pastor is a representative of the people and subject to their will.

After I resigned from the Lutheran School of Theology at Chicago in 1991, the year between the two "Call to Faithfulness" conferences, we moved to Northfield to found the Center for Catholic and Evangelical Theology. Since I was not at the age of retirement, 62 years, people were asking, why did I leave one of the most prestigious teaching positions in American Lutheran theological education, a chair in systematic theology once occupied by the esteemed Lutheran scholars, George Forell and Joseph Sitler. My friend, Robert Jenson, wrote an editorial in *Dialog* with the heading, "So Why Did Braaten Do It?"[26] This is what Jenson wrote, and he got it right. "The very reasons that took Carl into seminary teaching in the first place and made him persist so tenaciously have now taken him out. None other could have done it. He needs a place to serve the gospel and its church by the doing and teaching of theology. What made Carl Braaten overturn his life is a judgment: seminaries of the ELCA are now institutions emphatically inhospitable to theological work and instruction, and are likely to remain so for the foreseeable future." The future has arrived. Sad to say, not a single one of the ELCA seminaries is now a place were serious theological education for pastoral ministry is taking place.

WHAT IS THE CENTER FOR CATHOLIC AND EVANGELICAL THEOLOGY?

The two "Call to Faithfulness" conferences had an exclusively intramural Lutheran focus. The Center for Catholic and Evangelical in contrast was to focus on the extramural relations

---

26. Robert W. Jenson, "So Why Did Braaten Do It?" *Dialog, A Journal of Theology*, Volume 30, Autumn, 1991, 262-263.

between Lutheranism and the *Oecumene* — the whole church of Jesus Christ on earth. Unfortunately, since these two events happened at about the same time and in the same place, many in the church public, especially in positions of leadership, bishops and theologians, were confused about their difference. To get a clear picture of what the Center is all about, a Minneapolis church paper, the *Metro Lutheran*, asked Wilfred Bockelman, to interview Jenson and me. The interview expresses what we had in mind for the Center at its inception.

Wilfred Bockelman: "What is the Center for Catholic and Evangelical Theology and why did you start it?"

Robert Jenson: "Our name says it all. We are 'catholic' in the sense that we hold to the ecumenical creeds of the church; we are 'evangelical' because we believe that the Scriptures and those Creeds form the basis for the church's task of proclaiming the gospel, the evangel, in today's world. This Center was established by Lutherans in service of the ecumenical church."

Carl Braaten: "We have three major purposes — to promote theological research, to publish the journal, *Pro Ecclesia*, and theological monographs, and to sponsor colloquies and conferences for pastors and lay people. Close to the Center's core is a group of 20 who meet twice a year in what we call 'The Dogmatics Colloquium.' Its purpose is to bring together younger scholars to engage in research with an aim to publish, thus trying to forge new directions in theology. Frankly, we are trying to get a different kind of theology going in American Christianity, a kind that is faithful to the church's reading of the Scriptures, in continuity with the great Ecumenical Councils and the mainstream of the church's teaching in the Western Catholic and Eastern Orthodox traditions."

WB: "There is a perception around that you and your Center are pretty strongly anti-ELCA. Is that true and, if so, why?"

RJ: "When we were editors of the theological journal *Dialog*, we wrote many editorials critical of things in the ELCA. We have tried to make it clear, however, that the Center is not organized against the ELCA but has its own ecumenical purpose."

CB: "I am certainly not anti-ELCA, unless you identify ELCA with what goes on in the Chicago bureaucracy (the churchwide offices). I belong to the ELCA by choice and serve it. But I am definitely and openly against certain trends and policies pursued within the ELCA. The same things could be said about the Anglican (Episcopal) Church. We definitely know what the church ought to be doing and what it ought not be doing. No church should be organized the way the ELCA is organized. But our Center is not at all the medium to express such opinions and criticisms. The Center has a positive theological agenda and a distinct ecumenical orientation."

WB: "I heard that you tried to persuade the present board of *Dialog* to resign and allow you to choose your own board, and that the board defeated that move. Is that true?"

RJ: "Yes. Carl and I were chiefly responsible for starting *Dialog* over 30 years ago and served as its editors most of that time. But we both came to the conclusion that the original reason for creating *Dialog* no longer existed, and that we needed a different kind of journal."

CB: "Our proposal lost, 14 to 11. Had all the members of *Dialog*'s council been able to attend, the result might have been different. Council members do not get their way paid to attend meetings, so many don't come. Those who do are the ones from Luther Seminary in St. Paul, and Jens and I are out of sync with them in our understanding of ecumenical theology. When we started *Dialog*, Lutherans were pretty much stuck in their ethnic ghettoes. We felt we needed something like *Dialog* to engage the culture. But now we are in a totally different situation. Lutheranism doesn't need to be opened up to culture; it has been overtaken by culture. We need now to reopen the conversation with the great traditions of the church, reaching back to the ancient, medieval, and Reformation streams."

WB: "What conferences are you planning?"

CB: "We expect about 400 people from across the country and from all denominations to attend a conference in June at St. Olaf College on the theme, 'Reclaiming the Bible for the Church.' The conference will focus on the gaps between the historical-critical method of biblical studies and the doctrines of the church."

RJ: "We in no way believe in going back to the pre-critical approach to biblical interpretation. On the other hand, the method of critical exegesis has not proved to be sufficient. What happens to pastors is, they learn the historical-critical method and then have to preach on the text. Either they simply ignore what they learned or the method sort of cripples them, keeping them from having anything to say. Nobody has really figured out how to overcome this. We'll gather leading theologians, chosen ecumenically. All have the same assignment: 'What do you think can be done to overcome the gulf between what students learn about the Bible in the seminary and what they must do with it liturgically and homiletically when they become pastors?'"

WB: "Why did you choose to do the Center's work outside the structures of the church rather than within it?"

CB: "I do not think we could fulfill our mission inside the official structure. We are not bound to be politically correct. We are free to plan our projects without being controlled by the ELCA quota system. We are not a political lobby in the church with an activist agenda. We do not intend to devote our conferences to hot-button issues — sexuality, for instance. If we did that and a reporter were present, that would get the headlines and it wouldn't matter what anybody said about God, Christ, salvation, or anything else. So, knowing that American culture is obsessed with sex, we will be counter-cultural and talk about God."

The *Metro Lutheran* interview was too brief and spontaneous to provide a full description of the nature and purpose of the Center for Catholic and Evangelical Theology. We circulated a more complete description of the Center's mission to inform the general church public and especially like-minded individuals we were asking to join and support us in this venture. When we look back twenty five years later, we are humbled and grateful that by God's grace and the goodwill of many supporters the Center has been enabled to stay on track and realize a good portion of its dream. At the same time, looking back, we confess that some of what we dreamed to accomplish has proved to be unrealistic or beyond our reach.

STATEMENT OF PURPOSE

We mailed out thousands of brochures that contained the following information.

The Center for Catholic and Evangelical Theology is established to promote faithfulness throughout the church to the Word of God in Jesus Christ. The Center will seek to advance the knowledge of God's revelation as this is authoritatively mediated by Holy Scripture and normatively interpreted by the Ecumenical Creeds and Lutheran confessional writings. The Center is dedicated to the continuing education of ministers through research, conversation and publication. The Center is to be an independent resource in the service of the church and its ministries.

Karl Barth's *Church Dogmatics* began with these words: "Theology is a function of the church." Paul Tillich began his *Systematic Theology* in a similar way: "Theology is a function of the Christian church." We agree. But theology must serve in responsible freedom if it is to be true to its task of helping the church to be the church of Christ. Theology serves when it examines church tradition in the light of the gospel as well as when it subjects contemporary forms of Christian faith to evangelical criticism. In every age, we must ask what constitutes Christian faith, to grasp anew its basis and contents and not be misled by the attractions of current ideologies.

The Center for Catholic and Evangelical Theology will pursue policies intended to serve "the faith which was once for all delivered to the saints" (Jude 3). To this end the Center will:

1. Challenge and inspire the church to meet the crisis of Christian identity brought about whenever the gospel is mixed with elements of alien ideologies and religion;

2. Seek to retrieve neglected treasures of the catholic tradition, doctrinal, institutional and liturgical, in light of Reformation critique;

3. Engage in ecumenical research, to understand how various churchly traditions interpret and transmit the faith;

4. Seek to reclaim the normative application of the biblical-Christian ethic of obedient faith, in the Christian life and in the church's social witness.

BASIC AFFIRMATIONS

The Ecumenical Creeds of the ancient church provide us with a paradigm of Christian understanding based on the confession of Jesus Christ and the triune God, which we accept as definitive also for contemporary systematic and ecumenical theology. The following affirmations express the core of the Trinitarian and Christological faith of the church and are of crucial significance in a period of doctrinal relativism and norm-less pluralism.

1. Jesus Christ is the heart of God's unique and unsurpassable self-revelation in the history of humanity and the world.

2. The essence of the gospel is the apostolic message of the crucified and risen Lord from whom we have received the promise of salvation.

3. The Triune God, Father, Son and Holy Spirit, is an eternal communion of love at one with his saving acts in history "for us and for our salvation."

4. The church is the communion of those called through the gospel to participate in the life of the Triune God.

5. The Holy Spirit sustains the being and life of the church, and preserves it in true faith against false teaching.

6. The Holy Scriptures convey the ultimate truth of God's revelation in Christ and are thus the standard by which the church is to test all its teachings.

7. The Lutheran doctrine of justification by grace through faith alone is the "article by which the church stands or falls" because it conveys nothing other than the saving gospel of Jesus Christ.

8. The church as an instrument of the Kingdom of God is called to work for world peace and human well-being in all dimensions of life, but its unique and exclusive mission is to proclaim the gospel to all nations.

PROGRAMS

In order to realize the Center's commitment to the classical Christian tradition and to the Reformation, the Center will provide a variety of services and programs. Their focal point will be to promote the ongoing education of ministers for faithful service to Word and Sacraments. The Center will:

1. Offer continuing education courses for pastors in the classical theological disciplines;

2. Sponsor seminars on significant questions of theology now affecting the life of the church in its mission of the gospel;

3. Organize open theological conferences for reflection on Christian identity and mission in American Christianity;

4. Publish an occasional newsletter or bulletin to keep subscribers informed of coming events and to provide editorial commentary on the state of church and theology;

5. Publish a series of monographs for pastors, lay theologians, church leaders and seminarians;

6. Develop a network of persons who wish to be associated with the work of the Center, to participate in its projects and seminars, and to assist in its support;

7. Make its resources available to synods and regions, and to other centers of continuing education that aim to foster the evangelical and ecumenical vocation of congregations.

THE DOGMATICS PROJECT

The aim of this project will be to create a community of systematic theological stimulation, critique and work. The stated goal will be the production of a series of systematic theological monographs, under the editorship of the Center.

Twenty five participants will be invited, with a preponderance of younger thinkers. There are at present many of the latter, who show great promise that are subject to severe discouragement by the condition of their faculties and denominations. The group will be ecumenical, though it may be expected that a plurality will come from the Lutheran tradition.

The group will meet twice a year, for two full days on each occasion.

THE ECCLESIOLOGY SEMINAR

It has long been acknowledged that the theological task of the 20th century is the understanding of the church itself. The lack of such an understanding is the chief evil in the life of the various churches, and a chief barrier to ecumenical progress. The Center's first established senior seminar will appropriately take ecclesiology for its matter.

Twenty to thirty established scholars and thinkers will be invited. The group will be fully ecumenical, though perhaps at this stage not yet international.

The group will meet twice a year, for two days on each occasion. Papers will be presented to each meeting. The papers, and summaries of the discussion when appropriate, will be published, in a journal that will be established under separate identification and control but will be available to the Center's publications.

We received many responses from church leaders to our "Statement of Purpose." This is what the presiding bishop of the ELCA, Herbert W. Chilstrom, wrote in reply: "I wonder why we need such a center for theological studies. It occurs to me that everything you envision should, in fact, be among the purposes our theological seminaries seek to fulfill." He had a right to expect this of our seminaries, but Jenson and I, after having together experienced over 50 years of teaching in Lutheran seminaries, had come to expect otherwise.

William H. Lazareth, Bishop of Metropolitan New York Synod, offered a positive commendation: "I am convinced that it will prove to be a blessing for this church and beyond, and I therefore commend you for your courageous commitment to do theology as a function of the church."

Glenn W. Nycklemoe, Bishop of Southeastern Minnesota Synod, expressed the fears of many: "As a Bishop of the church, I would have a deep concern that it would not become a Center that fostered or even promoted any bashing of church leaders, the ELCA constitution, policies, and social statements."

Harold C. Skillrud, Bishop of Southeastern Synod wrote: "I recognize the need for what you are proposing and would support you in it. I am terribly bothered by what seems to be a perceptible drift away from our traditional confessional commitments, especially in the use of language and reference to the Triune God in worship and theological formulations."

Paull E. Spring, Bishop of Northwestern Pennsylvania Synod wrote: "Given our present situation, I applaud the effort you are engaged in. Perhaps a free-standing theological center will help the church to come to a fresh understanding of its life and mission."

Kenneth H. Sauer, Bishop of Southern Ohio Synod wrote: "I surely wish you and Jenson the best of success in this new work.... If the work that you and Jenson are embarking on can assist us to begin to make connections between our hearts, our heads, and our actual concrete churches, it could be very exciting."

It was clear to us from the many responses we received that most were under the mistaken impression that we would be primarily a renewal movement within Lutheranism, and some cautioned against the kind of church criticism and bashing they had come to associate with the "Call to Faithfulness" conferences. But that proved to be a needless worry because Jenson and I had vowed to discontinue our sharp diatribes directed against matters internal to the ELCA and American Lutheranism in general, as we had done in spades in the editorial pages of *Dialog*, the theological journal we edited for thirty years.

By our works we will be judged. Those who have attended the theological conferences sponsored by the Center, numbering over thirty five, have heard nary a word of ELCA-bashing, which would make no sense anyway, considering we have held our conferences in such places as St. Thomas University, St. John's University, Notre Dame University, Loyola College, Princeton Seminary, Duke Divinity School, Beeson Divinity School, proof positive that our Center from the start has had a full-orbed ecumenical orientation and purpose. And that, God-willing, is bound to continue.[27]

BANQUET ADDRESS, 2017

My most recent reflection on the birth and life of the Center for Catholic and Evangelical Theology was prepared as a banquet

---

27. For a more complete account of what the Center for Catholic and Evangelical Theology has accomplished in its first twenty five years, please see my theological biography, *Because of Christ, Memoirs of a Lutheran Theologian* (Grand Rapids, MI: Wm. B. Eerdmans Publishing Co., 2010), pp. 133-154.

address delivered at the annual theological conference of the Center, Loyola College, Baltimore, on the theme of "Repentance and Reconciliation." As a founder of the Center I was asked to be the banquet speaker to celebrate its 25th anniversary. I entitled my talk, "We Believe in the One Church of Jesus Christ." I devoted a good share of my speech to honor Robert W. Jenson, my friend and co-founder of the Center, for his many major contributions to its programs and publications. This occurred in June, 2017. Robert Jenson passed away three months later. Here are some excerpts of what I said.

"The Center was the product of half a century of a profound spiritual relationship between Robert Jenson and myself, as well as the deep collaboration of our spouses, Blanche and LaVonne. I will call him Jens, as those who love him most are wont to do. Jens and I were graduates of the same seminary — Luther Seminary in St. Paul, Minnesota. Soon thereafter we were both doctoral students at the University of Heidelberg, Germany. I was there to write my doctoral dissertation for Harvard Divinity School, with Paul Tillich as my doctor father. Jens received his doctorate from Heidelberg University, with Peter Brunner as his doctor father, after writing his dissertation on the theology of Karl Barth. We became life-long friends that year in Heidelberg. That laid the foundation of the kind of collegial activity that included the founding and editing of *Dialog — A Journal of Theology*, in 1962. Our collaborative friendship deepened in 1967, the year I studied at Oxford University on a Guggenheim Fellowship, where Jens was Dean and Tutor of Lutheran students at Mansfield College. Every weekend we would meet for Sherry Hour and dinner either at our house or at the Jensons, where the four of us would exchange notes of what we were thinking — and doing our best to solve the problems of the church and the world. That was the year that Martin Luther King and Bobby Kennedy were assassinated, and the year we found ourselves radicalized, joining Clergy and Laity opposed to the misguided Vietnam War, following the lead of Richard John Neuhaus."

I went on to describe the ensuing years of our collaborative efforts, the publication of two volumes of *Christian Dogmatics* that we co-edited, the two "Call to Faithfulness Conferences" that we organized, and then the founding of the Center for Catholic and Evangelical Theology in 1991.

"Jens and I had come to realize that in the twentieth century a great longing for Christian unity had been unleashed in all the churches and this longing is the work of the Holy Spirit. We had taken to heart the prayer of Jesus that 'they may all be one' so that 'the world might believe.' So what can we do, given our meager means? The strategy of the Center was to reclaim the great tradition of evangelical, catholic, and orthodox theology by bringing together the best theological minds in all the churches to join its colloquies, speak at its conferences, write for its journal *Pro Ecclesia,* and as the Center evolved, to serve on its Board of Directors. Today we have a strong ecumenically representative Board of Directors — Episcopalian, Presbyterian, Catholic, Orthodox, and Lutheran."

"When the Center was less than a decade old, it seemed important for us to go public on where we stand in the ecumenical movement, especially since institutional ecumenism, as represented by the World Council of Churches, had adopted a "new ecumenical paradigm" that called for a shift away from the concerns of "Faith and Order" to matters of social justice, care for the planet, and inter-religious dialogue. The upshot was a diminished focus on mission and evangelism. The Center was not about to go in that direction. Instead, we invited sixteen theologians and ecumenists representing various traditions to undertake an intensive study of the state of ecumenism. Members wrote background study papers for group discussion and published them in a book entitled, *The Ecumenical Future* (Eerdmans, 2004). It also drafted a manifesto of principles shared by the group, published under the title, *In One Body Through The Cross: The Princeton Proposal for Christian Unity* (Eerdmans, 2003). The ecumenical bureaucrats in Geneva did not look kindly at our criticisms, nor the kind of ecumenical future for which we were calling the churches to embrace."[28]

"I can well imagine that critics of the Center's ecumenical commitment might say, 'You guys are so old-fashioned.' That's true, in a way. Our ecumenical manifesto reaffirmed the 1961 statement of the World Council Assembly at New Delhi which described the church unity we seek as unity that 'is being made visible as all in each place who are baptized into Jesus Christ and confess him as Lord and Savior are brought by the Holy Spirit into one full committed fellowship, holding the one apostolic faith, preaching the one Gospel, breaking the one bread, joining in common prayer, and having a corporate life reaching out in witness and service to all and who at the same time are united with the whole Christian fellowship in all places and all ages, in such wise that ministry and members are accepted by all, and that all can act and speak as occasion requires for the tasks to which God calls his people.'"

"In my travels I have had the privilege of visiting many churches in Asia, Africa, and Latin America. I have witnessed the grace of Christ and the inspiring works of the Spirit way beyond the borders of the declining church to which I belong. I am not able to doubt that even within the churches officially separated from each other, as we say, not in altar and pulpit fellowship, the living Christ is present. We know that God desires the unity of the church, since Jesus prayed that all his followers may be one, yet we cannot stop his powerful Spirit from working in each of the churches that confess Jesus as Lord and Savior. We do not believe that Christ will allow churches separated from each other to exist in separation from him. In spite of their divisions they are one in Christ; they are members of the one body of Christ through baptism and faith. This unity may be hidden from the eyes of unbelief, but

---

28. We sent Cardinal Joseph Ratzinger a copy of *In One Body Through The Cross: The Princeton Proposal for Christian Unity* and received back from him a response of thanks, gratitude and assurance of his prayerful best wishes.

for those who believe, this unity is so real that everything that disfigures or contradicts this unity causes pain and summons them to come together at the ecumenical roundtable where, God willing, one day in eating and drinking together we can all celebrate the real presence of the crucified and risen Lord Jesus Christ. In the last fifty years Christians around the world, millions of them, belonging to many different churches, are visibly coming together at the grass roots, joining in prayer, worship, witness, and service, in spite of their official separation at headquarters. The presupposition of one church engaging another, whether in dialogue or service, is that the one, holy, catholic, and apostolic church is a reality in both of them."

I wrote the following words as the conclusion of my address, which at the same time encapsulate my abiding commitment to the ecumenical goal of full visible unity of the one church of Jesus Christ. I entitled my conclusion, "The Promised Land."

"The fact is, the ecumenical movement has been enormously successful. It is only one hundred years old. We don't have time to track all the differences it has made. But I do want to offer a vision for the future of ecumenism to which the Center for Catholic and Evangelical Theology might contribute in positive ways."

"We believe in the one holy catholic and apostolic church." 'We believe that the Holy Spirit calls, gathers, enlightens, and sanctifies the whole Christian church on earth, and keeps it united with Jesus Christ in the one true faith' (Luther's explanation to the Third Article of the Apostles' Creed). We would not be at work with this Center, if we did not believe this. It is also true that we would not have this Center, if everything was all right with the church. The church of Jesus Christ is divided, badly divided. Division is a sin and a disgrace. We believe in the oneness of the church. How can the church be united and divided at the same time? How can we, you and I, be holy and sinful at the same time? You can see that I am sneaking in Luther's concept of the *simul*. We are saints and sinners at the same time (*simul iustus et peccator*).²⁹ The church is holy and sinful at the same time. The church is holy because of Christ; the church is sinful because it is composed of people, all sinners like ourselves. The church is one, because it is the body of Christ, and Christ has only one body. And yet, at the same time, the church is not one; it is fractured, and each of us belongs to a fraction of the whole church. We will know when our churches become visibly one, when together we hear the living Word of God in proclamation, when together we see the active Word of God in baptism, when together we taste the presence of the Word of God in the Lord's Supper. Hearing, seeing, tasting — physical signs of the Real Presence of Christ. The gospel and the sacraments are the means by which the Holy Spirit creates the churches and incorporates them into the one body of Christ."

"We need to keep our eyes on the prize, no matter how far down the road the churches will need to go to attain it. We believe in nothing less than the goal of ecumenism affirmed by the New Delhi statement. Full visible church unity among the now separated churches will include basic agreement on matters of faith and doctrine. That's what the church-to-church dialogues continue to work on. That's the indispensable role that theology plays. That will continue to be a priority of this Center. That's why the Center will continue to sponsor theological conferences and colloquies as well as publish our theological quarterly, *Pro Ecclesia*, and a series of *Pro Ecclesia* monographs. We are so grateful to the editor of the journal, Joseph Mangina, and all who contribute to make *Pro Ecclesia* the great theological journal that it is."

---

29. I am aware that some churches do not accept Martin Luther's concept of the *simul*, the belief that a Christian after baptism is still a sinner. Try as I might, I am not able to grasp the objection that some Roman Catholics theologians have raised against the treatment of the *simul* in the "Joint Declaration on the Doctrine of Justification," signed by the Lutheran World Federation and the Pontifical Council for the Promotion of Christian Unity. If a Christian is not still a sinner after baptism, what is the point of confession, in which he or she asks God for forgiveness and absolution? It seems that the objection is a mere quibbling with words.

"We believe that theology matters, but it is not everything. Full visible church unity will necessarily also include life together in worship, prayer, evangelism, and works of mercy. It will also require recognition of the validity and reciprocity of each other's members and ministries wherever they may be serving. These are essential aspects of ecumenism that call for concrete action on the part of the various church bodies. Theology can help to create the conditions to make these aspects of church unity possible, but other agencies will need to take the lead. The Center is a theological organization. Insofar as serious theology in many of our church institutions is going over the cliff like the Gadarene swine, our mission is to keep the ecumenical movement moving forward in the right direction. Even though the churches are not yet united, they are no longer against each other like they have been for centuries. They are now more and more acting with each other and in good faith praying for each other. Just think what it meant when Pope Francis joined the Catholic-Lutheran commemoration of the Reformation in Sweden, urging reconciliation and cooperation. Similar commemorations are happening in thousands of cities and churches throughout the world, and there will be no turning back the clock."

"We at the Center are thankful that we can be part of this miracle of the twenty first century. Our mission is to hasten the growth of the unity that God has in store for the churches and is bringing it about through his Holy Spirit.... The first step that each church and each of us must take is self-examination leading to repentance. And the next step to reconciliation is readiness to forgive. When the churches do this *coram deo*, each of them will be delivered from the evil of thinking of itself as the center around which the other churches orbit. If we truly seek reconciliation through repentance and forgiveness, we must take our starting point with Christ, by whom all churches are to be judged and measured. He alone is the Sun around whom the churches revolve as planets and from whom we see the light that shines in the darkness of our world. That is the kind of 'Copernican revolution' that Professor Edmund Schlink called for in his review of the Second Vatican Council of which he was an official observer from the Evangelical Church in Germany.[30] We pray that this concept will guide the ecumenical vision of the Center for Catholic and Evangelical Theology in the years to come."

The year 2017 has drawn to a close. It will be remembered as the year that commemorated, if not indeed celebrated, the 500th anniversary of the start of the Reformation when Martin Luther wrote his 95 theses, commonly thought to have been posted on the door of the Castle Church in Wittenberg, Germany. I was privileged to be able to contribute in a small way by giving a few lectures on the Reformation. They make up the rest of the story of my ecumenical journey beginning in 1965, when I gave my first ecumenical lecture on the tragedy of the Reformation (chapter 2 of this book). Part two of this book contains the lectures I gave to commemorate the Reformation, given to Lutherans in Charlotte, North Carolina and Anglicans in Dallas, Texas.

---

30. Edmund Schlink, "After the Council," in *Ecumenical and Confessional Writings*, edited by Matthew L. Becker (Vandenhoek & Ruprecht, 2017).

PART TWO
THE 500TH ANNIVERSARY OF THE REFORMATION

CHAPTER 4
WE BELIEVE IN THE ONE HOLY CATHOLIC AND APOSTOLIC CHURCH

In Chapter Two I wrote about my first ecumenical address to a pastoral conference in Illinois which offered a Lutheran assessment of the Second Vatican Council. The news reports of my talk went viral. Newspapers from coast to coast ran the story under the headline, "Braaten calls for return to Rome." The *Christian Century* weighed in with a strong rebuke, calling it "Protestant Hara-Kiri," Japanese for suicide. With the help of a few veteran ecumenical theologians the brouhaha was put to rest as what is now called "fake news," and the editor of the magazine had to modify its story.

That inauspicious entrance into the ecumenical controversies of the 20th century had for me one happy result. I gained a life-long friend in Pastor Michael McDaniel, who later became the Bishop of the North Carolina Synod of the ELCA. At this Reformation conference I wish to give this lecture in honor of the esteemed life and ministry of my friend, Mike McDaniel. He was one of the bishops of the ELCA who invited me on several occasions to address the pastors of his Synod. A number of the chapters of my book, *The Apostolic Imperative, Nature and Aim of the Church's Mission and Ministry*, are verbatim presentations of what I said at his pastoral conferences. I was also privileged to give a lecture at one of his Luther-Aquinas Conferences, comparing Catholic and Lutheran interpretations of the Bible.[31] Bishop McDaniel was a fearless champion of sound theology in a church that was replacing it with a world-conforming social agenda.

Many of us were busy in 2017 participating in occasions like this to celebrate the 500th anniversary of the Reformation, not knowing how much longer there will be anything left to celebrate, considering the downward spiral of the mainline Protestant denominations in Europe and North America. But I do not wish to start on a sour note. Rather, I wish to speak hopefully about the one church of Jesus Christ of which both Lutherans and Catholics are members, along with a great host of Protestant and Orthodox Christians and Churches. All churches that accept the creeds of the ancient church confess belief in the "One holy catholic and apostolic church." Whether we are Protestant or Catholic, Lutheran or Reformed, Western or Eastern, first world or third world, whatever the adjective, if we are true believers in Jesus Christ, we are members of his one body, and therefore belong to the one holy catholic and apostolic church. But do we really believe this? Do we act like we believe it? Do Christians from the myriad denominations — some estimate as many as 40,000 — behave toward each other as people belonging to one and the same body — the body of Christ?

The belief in the *una sancta catholica et apostolica* became a burden of conscience for Christians in the 20th century. To confess it became something of an embarrassment, especially for those who bore the burden of bringing the gospel to the non-Christian world. We are told that in the early church pagans would look at Christians and remark, "Look how they love one

---

31. Carl E. Braaten, "A Shared Dilemma: Catholics and Lutherans on the Authority and Interpretation of Scripture," *Pro Ecclesia* 10, No. 1 (Winter 2001), 63-75.

another." That could not be said of Lutherans and Catholics when I grew up on the mission field in Madagascar.

When I joined a group of Christians touring China in the early eighties, we would see a church steeple and ask our guide, Mr. Chi, "What kind of church is that?" He would say, "That is a Catholic church," meaning a Roman Church, or he would say, "That is a Christian church," meaning a Protestant church. Catholics and Protestants did not recognize each other as belonging to the one church of Jesus Christ, and they still don't. The same thing happened on the mission fields, throughout Asia, Africa, and South America, not only the division between Protestants and Catholics, but also between major blocs of Protestants. Anglicans made Anglicans of Nigerians; Lutherans made Lutherans of Tanzanians; Baptists made Baptists of the people of India; Presbyterians made Presbyterians of South Koreans. All the denominations made carbon copies of themselves, more or less, wherever they planted the church. Evangelization, that is, the worldwide missionary movement, went hand in hand with Western colonialism, replicating the divided churches of the "first world" among the colonized peoples of the so-called "third world." That is what is meant by the scandal of church division.

THE BIRTH OF THE ECUMENICAL MOVEMENT

But then something remarkable happened. A new Pentecostal outburst of the Holy Spirit inspired missionary church leaders to begin the quest for Christian unity. Thus the ecumenical movement can be said to have been born on the mission field, most notably giving birth to the Church of South India, a union of Anglican, Methodist, Presbyterian, and Congregational Churches. Lutherans were involved in the early negotiations but dropped out, I heard, because their financial ties to their partner churches in Europe and America would be cut off. Money talks where it shouldn't. The new church chose as its motto the prayer of Jesus in John 17:21: "That they may all be one, even as thou, Father, art in me, and I in thee, that they may also be in us, so that the world may believe that thou hast sent me." The mission churches came to realize — not for theoretical reasons but for the sake of advancing the gospel on the ground — that the church of Jesus Christ must be one so that the world might believe. Ecumenism and evangelization were from that point on joined at the hip.

The World Council of Churches, Faith and Order, and other ecumenical organizations were founded to become the institutional instruments to translate the prayer of Jesus into the historical reality we are experiencing here and now. We are truly blessed that we have the privilege of living our Christian faith in an ecumenical era, coming out of our denominational ghettoes, entering into multilateral conversations and collaboration, even giving hope in some quarters that our separate churches would go one step further to institutional consolidation. The rendezvous of churches after Vatican II stimulated hope that we would all move to one universal church structure, perhaps one global bureaucracy, though no one dared to breathe that Geneva would serve better than Rome. Today such a dream of one institutionalized church bureaucracy has been shattered beyond recovery, thanks be to God! Fifty some years of ecumenical dialogues have brought Christians and churches closer together but they have not succeeded in uniting the divided churches of Christendom. The stumbling block has been and still is, churches cannot agree on what model of unity Jesus had in mind when he prayed that his followers "may all be one." What does it mean to be one? What has to happen to make it happen? Catholics and Lutherans still cannot eat and drink together at the one Table of the Lord. When they reach that point, they will experience, in my view, the *sine qua non* of real Christian unity.

At the same time that the major denominations have failed to realize the dream of a great family reunion, they have fallen into internal strife. The divisions within the mainline churches have become more painful than those that come between them. Schisms have recently occurred among Episcopalians, Presbyterians, and Lutherans, to name a few. The church of Jesus Christ throughout history has not learned how to be and remain united in the midst of controversy. Schisms have occurred over biblical authority and inerrancy, over baptism and the Lord's Supper, over predestination and free will, over episcopal succession and papal infallibility, over human sexuality and the definition of marriage. So where does that leave us? It leaves us with a divided church and the absence of unity.

If we look at the second attribute of the church, the holiness of the church, we face the same conundrum. As Karl Rahner put it so succinctly, "We are a church of sinners!" Yes, every last one of us, from the Pope on down to the lowliest *hoi polloi*. Yet, we do confess the holiness of the church every Sunday. Which leads us to ask, "What can this possibly mean, when the plain reality is exactly the opposite?" Our task is to explain this confessional statement, "We believe in the only holy catholic and apostolic church." I do not want to surrender this confession of the Nicene Creed, even though it seems to be on its face a statement contrary to fact. Where is the one church? Of what does it consist? Where is the holy church? Of what does it consist? And so forth.

Let us start at the beginning. How did these four heavy-laden words — one holy catholic and apostolic — get into the Creed, inasmuch as they are not in the Bible? Nowhere in the New Testament is the church described by these four adjectives. The words "catholic" and "apostolic" never appear at all, and while the words "one" and "holy" are found in many contexts, there is no reference to the "one holy church." This sort of observation has led some Christians and even denominations to make do without the creeds of the church. "No Creeds but Christ" is the slogan of one American church body.

I have to confess that I grew up in a church that did not use the Nicene Creed in Sunday worship services, only the Apostles'

Creed. The Nicene Creed does not appear in Luther's *Small Catechism*, which like so many of you, I had to memorize word for word. Therefore, the words, "one holy catholic and apostolic," did not get cemented into my theological vocabulary until later. I grew up among Norwegian American Lutheran pietists, missionaries in Madagascar, and though they planted a vital church among the Malagasy people, they did not teach a high doctrine of the church — mostly low church. I did often hear, the church is "where two or three are gathered in my name, there am I in the midst of them" (Matt. 18:20). But that is not meant to be a definition of the church.

When I took up the study of theology at Luther Seminary in St. Paul in 1952, my dream was to be the best possible Lutheran theologian I could. After years of graduate school at the University of Harvard and then Heidelberg, Germany, where the greatest Lutheran faculty of theology in modern times was assembled, my horizon was still limited to become the best possible Lutheran systematic theologian that God gave me the heart and brains to become. After all, I had been marinated in the juices of Lutheran preaching and teaching, piety and parish life. The word "ecumenism" never crossed my lips. But I do remember an eye-opening sermon preached by the great Methodist missionary to India, E. Stanley Jones, when I was a fledgling seminary student. He told about the many churches witnessing to Christ in India. Rather than looking at them as competitors, he preferred to see them as complementary, with each of them bringing a special God-given gift to the missionary enterprise. The Anglicans bring their appreciation for liturgical worship, Presbyterians their concern for church order, Methodists their stress on holy living, Lutherans their belief in pure doctrine, Baptists their zeal for pioneer evangelism, and so forth. Then he summed it up, saying, "In conversion you are not attached primarily to an order, nor an institution, nor a movement, nor a set of beliefs, nor a code of conduct — you are attached primarily to a Person and secondarily to these other things."

THE ONENESS OF THE CHURCH

That is exactly right, the clue to a right interpretation of our belief in the one holy catholic and apostolic church. The confession about the church is paradoxical because it seems to contradict what our ordinary eyes can see. That is why we say, "We believe"; it's a matter of faith, not sight. Before we confess our belief in the church, we have first confessed our faith in Jesus Christ, the only begotten Son of God, true God and true man. It is solely on account of Christ that we confess the church is one. The church is one because it is the body of Christ. There are many church bodies, but Christ has only one. There are many members of the one body of Christ, as the apostle Paul says in his Letter to the Romans and the Galatians. If you believe in Jesus as God's anointed Messiah, and are baptized into the name of the Holy Trinity, you are a member of the body of Christ. What makes the church you belong to a part of the one church of Jesus Christ does not depend on any particular attribute your particular church likes to boast about. It depends exclusively on its radical dependence on the unifying gospel of Jesus Christ. The essence of the church lies in its relation to Jesus Christ, and hence to God the Father and the Holy Spirit, recipient by grace of all the works of the Holy Trinity.

The place to recharge our ecumenical batteries is in face of the Christological question, "Who is Jesus of Nazareth?" The ecumenical movement stands or falls with the original question of Jesus to his disciples on the road to Caesarea Philippi, "Who do you say that I am?" The core of the church's unity and universality lies in its relation to the Person of Jesus Christ and his gospel, and that is sufficient, as we confess in Article VII of the *Augsburg Confession*. "Our (Lutheran) churches teach that the one holy church is to continue forever. The church is the assembly of saints in which the Gospel is taught purely and the sacraments are administered rightly. For the true unity of the church it is enough (*satis est*) to agree concerning the teaching of the Gospel and the administration of the sacraments. It is not necessary that human traditions or rites and ceremonies, instituted by men, should be alike everywhere." This means that everything going on in the church must conform to the gospel of Jesus Christ. Every interpretation of Scripture, every creed, cult or office must function as a sign and instrument of the whole gospel of Christ. And they do; that is how the "Great Tradition" of classical Christianity developed and that is why the challenge of every generation is to pass it on to the next. Whatever piece of church tradition does not express the once-for-all revelation of God in Jesus Christ is an *adiaphoron* — a non-essential — something we can take or leave. The converse is also true: whatever piece of church tradition that provides a true witness to the mystery of Christ is something to be cherished and celebrated. It's what makes us catholic, not Roman Catholic, but catholic in the sense of retaining continuity with the whole church of Christ in history and today.

When we Lutherans confess that for church unity "it is enough that we agree on the teaching of the Gospel," we have in mind the whole gospel that includes Christ and the Church. The church is part of the gospel, because Christ is the head of the church and the church is the body of Christ. The head and the body belong together, indivisibly, inseparably, forming the whole Christ. They are one, and that is why we believe in the one church. There is nothing we can do to make the church one. The church is already one in Christ. The mission of the ecumenical movement is to help the various churches to show it more. That is what churches joining each other in dialogue and service is all about -- to find better ways of showing our unity in the Christ of the gospel so that the world might believe.

Does it bother you, as it does me, when any given church proclaims itself to be the one and only church of Jesus Christ? Just like it irritates me when one nation boasts of being the best in the world. That reminds me of kids on a playground bragging that my dad can beat up on your dad.

THE HOLINESS OF THE CHURCH

As for the holiness of the church, we have already admitted the sinfulness of the church. There is no church without "spot or wrinkle" (Eph. 5:27). Again, as with the oneness of the church, the fulness of the church resides in Christ and Christ alone. As members of his body we are called to be holy, and we believe the Holy Spirit is working full time to sanctify every member of the body of Christ. As with every Christian justified by faith alone, in Christ a "wonderful exchange" takes place, as Luther phrased it, his righteousness for our sinfulness. Every day we pray in the *Lord's Prayer* for the forgiveness of sins. And the next day we start over and struggle to bring forth the fruits of faith pleasing to God.

I recall how shocked I was when a college classmate of mine returned from a weekend spiritual retreat in Minnesota and thanked God that he was now sinless. He had received the spiritual gift of entire sanctification, of sinless perfection, the so-called baptism of the Holy Spirit. I asked him if he remembered the story about the Pharisee and the tax collector. The Pharisee prayed, "God, I thank thee that I am not a sinner like those others." By contrast the tax collector prayed, "God, be merciful to me a sinner." Those without sin have no need for a Savior. Those who are not sick have no need for a physician.

A Lutheran theologian does not often quote a Reformed Confession, but one can hardly say it better than the *Westminster Confession*, which states, "The purest churches under heaven are subject to mixture and error." This expresses John Calvin's idea that the church is a *corpus mixtum*, a mixed body of both good and bad, and Lutherans would chime in with, both "righteous and sinful" (*simul iustus et peccator*) at the same time. Today it is easier to believe in the sinfulness of the church than in its holiness. Newspaper headlines love to publicize the heresies of bishops, the transgressions of TV-evangelists, and the sexual misconduct of priests, costing the church billions of dollars and forcing some dioceses to declare bankruptcy.

Let those who have no sin cast the first stone. Since the church is made up of people like us, we do confess that the church is a mixed bag. Perhaps you have friends who tell you that they don't go to church because it is full of hypocrites. When I hear that, I respond, "True, but that's like saying I won't go to a hospital because it is full of sick people." We go to church to join a company of sinners who need to repent, receive forgiveness, and promise to mend our ways. As an aside, perhaps we all remember a candidate recently running for high office who said he never asks God for forgiveness. He said, "I think if I do something wrong, I just try to make it right. I don't bring God into the picture."

So, yes, we will continue to confess that the church is holy, not because we are holy, but solely on account of Christ, who imparts his righteousness to the sin sick members of his body. Does it make sense? It's a paradox. The apostle Paul says the church is "a mystery" (Eph. 5:32). The church is holy and sinful at the same time, holy because of Christ, and sinful because we are its members.

THE CHURCH CATHOLIC

The most controversial attribute of the church is next. The church is catholic. This attribute of the church has been misunderstood by both Protestants and Catholics. Many Protestants refuse to use the term at all. They prefer to say "Christian" in reciting the Creed rather than "Catholic." They have surrendered the word "catholic" to the Church of Rome. That is understandable in a way because many Roman Catholics have claimed the exclusive right to the term for their own church. The word is in the Creed, our creed, so there is no good reason to give it up. The word "catholic" means "universal." Though the word is not in the New Testament, its meaning is clearly present in Jesus' Great Commission to the apostles in Matthew 28, to go and tell the gospel to all the world, to all the nations. The word "catholic" refers to the whole world — global, universal, from the Greek "*kata holos,*" according to the whole. If you do not belong to the catholic church, you belong to a sect or a cult. Like it or not, that's the reality.

St. Ignatius was the first to apply the word "catholic" to the church, at the beginning of the second century. You can find it in a letter Bishop Ignatius wrote to the Christians at Smyrna while on his journey to Rome to face martyrdom. If your church believes in spreading the gospel of the kingdom of Christ throughout the world, then your church is as catholic as any other. It simply belongs to the nature of the church to witness to Christ to everyone, everywhere, and always. The world-wide missionary enterprise began when the apostles received the power of the Holy Spirit at Pentecost. We believe in the catholic church because we are committed to the universal mission of the world-transforming gospel of Jesus Christ. I tried to teach my students two things about this: please, don't eliminate the word "catholic" from your confession of the church, and please, don't give in to the self-serving propaganda of any church that claims the attribute of catholicity exclusively for itself.

THE APOSTOLIC CHURCH

The fourth attribute of the church is my favorite. The church is apostolic or it is not the church of Jesus Christ. Jesus said, "I will build my church" (Matt. 16:18). He built it on the foundation of the apostles, with himself as its chief cornerstone. The apostolic church handed down to us seven fundamental characteristics that have belonged to the church from the beginning until now. Anyone who has studied a little bit of Greek is probably familiar with a few Greek words — seven in all — which have become part of every student's theological lexicon: *kerygma, martyria, didache, koinonia, diakonia, leiturgia, and paradosis.* From the apostles we have received the *kerygma.* The *kerygma* is the New Testament word for the gospel message preached by the apostles concerning the life, death, and resurrection of Jesus Christ. The apostles gave us their testimony, their witness to Christ, their *martyria*. They were martyrs for Christ, because of the witness they bore to him. We have received their *didache*, the didactic teachings of the apostles. We have been included in their *koinonia*, the fellowship of the apostles gathering for prayer and the breaking of bread. And the apostles made *diakonia* a fundamental part of the Christian life, the caring diaconal ministry of the church to the poor and oppressed. That is the gospel in action. The apostles called the people of Christ together for *leiturgia*, the worship of the people of God, their liturgy. We have received all these marvelous gifts from the tradition — the *paradosis* — of the apostles, and that is why we believe in the apostolic church. When Lutherans repeat the slogan, "Word alone," they do not mean without tradition. Our theologians interpret Scripture in light of the living stream of the great tradition of the church where the Holy Spirit has been active since Pentecost. One of my teachers, E. Clifford Nelson, a Lutheran church historian, once said something I have never forgotten, "Church history is the autobiography of the Holy Spirit."

Why should we care about such attributes of the church? Why are they important for us today? Martin Luther worried a lot about whether the church in his time was being faithful to its Christ-given apostolic nature. He asked, in effect, "How can a person tell a true church from a false church?" We live in a highly mobile society. Very few of us live in the same place our entire lifetime. When a family moves to a new city, the question becomes urgent, "How do I find a church I can trust, a church I am confident will pass on the true Christian faith in its fulness to my children and grand-children?" Already in the second century this became a crucial question. There were Christians who touted their belief in Christ, and were impressively spiritual. Irenaeus and Tertullian were two church fathers who wrote books against the heresy of gnosticism. The gnostic churches rejected the Old Testament, the God of creation, the God of Israel, the God who gave Moses the Ten Commandments. Instead, they wanted to know only the God of the New Testament, only the God of salvation, Christ the Redeemer, and experience their freedom in the gospel, freedom from obedience to the Jewish law. They were the first anti-Semites; they were "antinomians" — against the law. The message of freedom sounded very appealing. It beguiled many well-intentioned people in quest of a relevant spirituality. We are in the same boat today. Many in the new generation of millennials say, "We don't go to church, but we are spiritual." The New Age spirituality promises that you can know and experience God by turning inward, by getting in touch with your deepest self. But it is a false gospel. It was Freud — no church father he — who taught, the deeper you delve into yourself, the murkier and muckier things become.

It has been my privilege to travel in many parts of the world, to meet Christians and churches on every continent except Antarctica, to study and teach in many countries and schools where missionaries planted the church. Quite naturally, the first thing I try to do is to learn the state of the church and to find a place to worship. You can take the temperature of a church by attending its worship services. I have always been most pleased to find churches that are evangelical in mission, orthodox in doctrine, and joyful in worship. I have attended churches that preach about bunnies and springtime on Easter Sunday. That won't do it! But here is what I am looking for — an assembly that is centered in the Word of God, seasonal readings from Scripture, sermons that proclaim the message of God's law and gospel, the whole counsel of God, weekly gathering around the Table of the Lord, partaking of the life-giving soul food of bread and wine, and participating in doxological acts of praise and thanksgiving. We are talking about the quintessential practices of proclaiming the Word and administering the Sacraments. Of course, these things are done differently from place to place. High church, low church, or broad church, just so it's real church, that's all that matters. The attributes of the church make no sense without these practices. And when they are performed faithfully, they generate a spirit of welcoming to strangers, of sharing the staples of life to those in need, and collaboration with fellow Christians to preach the gospel to those who do not yet believe.

Luther said, "A seven year old child knows what the church is, namely, holy believers and sheep who hear the voice of the Shepherd." He was reacting to people who make things too complicated, by adding this or that, perhaps a particular style of worship, organizational structure, type of piety, or code of ethics. No, the church is where Christ is really present through Word and Sacrament in the power of the Spirit. After fifty years of ecumenical dialogues the churches are still divided. May it be that some church leaders and their theological advisers are making things too complicated? Lutherans have traditionally demanded doctrinal consensus as a prerequisite to altar and pulpit fellowship with other churches. Anglicans have traditionally required agreement on the so-called historic episcopacy. Roman Catholics still insist on nothing less than acknowledgment of papal primacy and authority. Going forward along these tracks, the ecumenical quest for church unity has hit the wall. At the July 2016 ELCA national assembly in New Orleans, the voting members approved a declaration of thirty two propositions on which Lutherans and Catholics agree, but the all important points of difference remain, most notably the dogma of papal infallibility.[32]

CHURCH UNITY AND DOCTRINAL CONSENSUS

Our traditional Lutheran requirement of full doctrinal consensus remains an obstacle not only between Lutherans and other denominations, but also between Lutheran Synods. We would have no trouble finding thirty propositions on which we could agree with the Lutheran Church-Missouri Synod or any other Synod, but once we take up matters such as biblical inerrancy or women's ordination, the conversation comes to an abrupt halt.

---

32. *Declaration on the Way: Church, Ministry and Eucharist* was developed by the ecumenical committees of the Evangelical Lutheran Church in America and the United States Conference of Catholic Bishops, 2015.

We may agree to disagree, but we are no closer to celebrating our unity in Christ at the Lord's Table. If doctrinal consensus is necessary for inter-communion, the question is bound to arise, "How much?" Some will say of a particular set of statements, "That's enough," but others will say, "More is necessary." So back to the merry-go-round of negotiations that never ends. Every church seems to have its favorite conversation stopper.

After being a close observer of the most important bi-lateral and multi-lateral dialogues, my personal judgment is that the churches are ill-advised to base the unity they seek on a new series of doctrinal statements subscribed by all in the same way. Lutherans have quibbled whether to subscribe their Confessions insofar as (*quatenus*) or because (*quia*) they conform to the Holy Scriptures. I cannot remember which philosopher coined the phrase about a proposition, but it may be apropos here — "dying the death of a thousand qualifications." Lutherans and Roman Catholics in the United States have published eleven volumes of dialogues, the first one on the Nicene Creed in 1965, and yet they don't seem to have brought us closer to eucharistic fellowship. In most ELCA congregations Roman Catholics are welcomed to Holy Communion, whereas Lutherans are officially excluded from sharing communion in Catholic parishes. The ecumenical movement has brought us a long way to friendlier relations, but not far enough for eating and drinking together at the Table of the Lord.

In my view church bodies that are open to sharing the same altars and pulpits are practicing the essence of church unity. They may not have the same confessional statements and creedal doctrines on every point, but in ecumenical dialogue they do examine each other's traditions sufficient to determine that they believe, teach, and preach the one gospel of Jesus Christ as the final hope of salvation, without necessarily producing a new common confession in language familiar to neither side. Christians and churches have discovered signs of unity, including the study of the same Scriptures, worshipping the same Christ, working toward the same goals, being open in love on a purely human plane, and suffering martyrdom at the hands of the same tyrants. We may sing different tunes and speak in strange dialects in expressing our thoughts of faith, but the glorious face of Christ and truth of the gospel can shine through nevertheless. That is what we have personally experienced ecumenically, and I feel sorry for churches that refuse to get on board the ecumenical train.

We can rejoice that many churches other than Lutheran are celebrating the 500th anniversary of the Reformation, and also giving thanks to God for the last fifty years of ecumenical experience. Lutherans are among those who have been at the forefront of the ecumenical movement. We remember with gratitude the service of the great ecumenical leaders such as Archbishop Nathan Söderblom and Professor Anders Nygren of Sweden, Professors Regin Pretner and Kirsten Skydsgaard of Denmark, Bishop Hanns Lilje and Professor Edmund Schlink of Germany, President Franklin Clark Fry and Professor George Lindbeck of the United States, just to mention a few. There are scores of others, Lutheran bishops and theologians, from Germany, Scandinavia, and the United States, who have been guided by the *Augsburg Confession* in their ecumenical work, practicing an ecumenism of the gospel. That's the Lutheran thing, judging everything — good or bad, right or wrong, true or false — by the criterion of the gospel of Jesus Christ. It's because of this that I have never dreamed of being or becoming anything other than a card carrying evangelical catholic of the *Augsburg Confession*, and it truly boggles my mind when I see fellow Lutherans swimming the Tiber or crossing some other boundary to leave behind the great traditions arising from the Lutheran Reformation. Only the gospel of Jesus Christ is the resource for renewing ecumenical activity with integrity.

The gospel, and only the gospel, proclaims the love of God, the flaming love that unites the Father and the Son and the Holy Spirit, the love which has come down to earth in baby Jesus and who welcomes us in baptism to be one with him, his sisters and brothers. The love of Jesus is the power of true unity because it overcomes oppositions and separations. How can we say we love Jesus if we play the game of solitaire, entrenched in our smug self-sufficiency, keeping apart from other members of the same family? A true celebration of the Reformation releases the pressure of God's love to seek communion with other Christians without demanding conformity, to seek unity without uniformity, and this is happening, thanks to the ecumenical movement, without planning for more mergers of the organizational bureaucratic sort.

Not so long ago it was said that the churches must unite in one visible church body because the world is scandalized by different denominations with their different labels and logos. I don't think the world is scandalized by diversity. The world has gotten used to the supermarket variety of things, and hardly expects religion to be any different. General Motors features a healthy competition between its various models — Chevrolets, Buicks, and Cadillacs. Diversity is good, only division is bad. We are all scandalized by the volumes of sins against the eighth commandment, starting with the religious wars between Protestants and Catholics after the Reformation. "Thou shalt not bear false witness against your neighbor." Luther asked, "What does this mean?" He answered, "We are to fear and love God, so that we do not tell lies about our neighbors, betray or slander them, or destroy their reputations. Instead we are to come to their defense, speak well of them, and interpret everything they do in the best possible light."

The ecumenical movement has brought us half way home. We are not sinning against each other as much as we used to, and we are enjoying it less. We are not protesting as much as we used to, possibly because the reason and passion for protest has virtually vanished from Protestantism, foreseeing what Paul Tillich seventy years ago called "the end of the Protestant era." We are at an ecumenical crossroads, wondering about the future of the Protestant Reformation, even whether God will give it any future worth celebrating. Maybe our Lord is telling us to direct our protestations against ourselves, worrying more about the log in our own eye than the speck in the eye of the other.

But at the moment we are here to thank God for the Spirit of love working miracles in the one body of Christ, with its members learning to convene, converse, and cooperate in more harmonious ways. The emerging unity is of the Spirit of God, filling the hearts of Christian people with the gospel of love. I will close with some words from Martin Luther's explanation of the Third Article of the Creed: "The Holy Spirit calls, gathers, enlightens, and makes holy the whole Christian Church on earth and keeps it with Jesus Christ in the one common, true faith." And then also the closing words of Jesus' high priestly prayer: "I made known to them thy name, and I will make it known, that the love with which thou hast loved me may be in them, and I in them" (John 17:26). Here in truth lies our hope for a renewed ecumenism — the gospel of love — for the sake of the greater realization of the one holy catholic and apostolic church on earth.

CHAPTER 5

THE PERMANENT SIGNIFICANCE OF THE REFORMATION FOR THE CHURCH

Lutherans have been seriously engaged in ecumenical dialogues since the Second Vatican Council — that's over fifty years — both at the world level and in the United States. The one thing no partner in dialogue could have missed — Lutheranism is synonymous with the doctrine of justification through faith alone apart from the works of the law. This happens by God's grace alone and solely on account of Christ. Some haven't liked the word "alone" — in Latin "sola" — but they have come to understand and even accept what Lutherans mean by it. Lutherans do not mean that only faith matters and that the doing of good works is good for nothing. Moreover, Lutherans have insisted that the doctrine of justification is the "article by which the church stand or falls," by which we mean not merely the Lutheran Church but the whole Church — the one, holy, catholic, and apostolic church of Jesus Christ. Our partner churches in dialogue have gotten the point. Lutherans are serious about it. They have upped the ante to the nth degree.

In this address I want to make three points. First, the doctrine of justification by faith alone lies at the heart of Luther's theology and of the Lutheran Confessions. Take that away and everything collapses like a house of cards. Second, the doctrine of justification is not merely a Lutheran thing, a peculiarity that Lutherans can keep in their private chest. Rather, it articulates the truth of the gospel of Jesus Christ for the whole church. Otherwise Lutheranism would be just another sect, one of a thousand, and if that's the case, I know that Martin Luther would say, "Let's just forget about it." And I would agree with that. Justification by faith alone apart from the works of the law is not a sectarian doctrine. And third, the doctrine of justification cannot stand alone like the fabulous cheese. It must be correlated with the church, or it doesn't have a leg to stand on. One thing Lutherans have learned in their ecumenical dialogues, if they didn't know it already, is that the church is the sign and instrument of God's plan of salvation for the whole world. Justification and the church are inseparably joined in a mutual relationship.

THE ESSENCE OF THE REFORMATION: JUSTIFICATION THROUGH FAITH ALONE

It is beyond dispute among the best scholars of today that Luther's encounter with the apostle Paul's theology of the righteousness of God lay at the heart of his liberating breakthrough experience enshrined in Article 4 of the *Augsburg Confession* concerning justification: "Our churches teach that human beings cannot be justified before God by their own powers, merits, or works. But they are justified as a gift on account of Christ through faith when they believe that they are received into grace and their sins are forgiven on account of Christ, who by his death made satisfaction for our sins. God reckons this faith as righteousness."

Luther's attack on the sale of indulgences escalated to an attack on the authority of the Pope and that provoked severe criticism from Luther's opponents, such as Johan Tetzel, John Eck and Cardinal Cajetan. They did not grasp the depth of Luther's discovery of the liberating gospel of justification. The fuss over indulgences and papal authority did not reveal at once that Luther's passion and concern was the liberating gospel of justification. Luther wrestled not only with the Letters of Paul, Galatians and Romans, but also with the writings of Augustine. The four *solas* framed his theology the years immediately following the publication of the 95 Theses — *solus Christus* or Christ alone, *sola gratia* or grace alone, *sola fide* or faith alone, and to buttress his defense of these *solas* over against his papal critics, he added to the equation *sola scriptura* or Scripture alone. When push comes to shove, neither the Pope nor the tradition of the Church has the last word, only Scripture does. The ultimate authority is the revelation of God in Holy Scripture on account of its gospel message of salvation — justification of sinners by the grace of God received through faith on account of Christ.

The stress on the primacy of Scripture does not mean the Creeds and Councils of the Church have no authority. Luther was not a radical reformer who rejected church tradition. He was criticized by other reformers for not going far enough to reject the traditional rites, ceremonies, sacraments, festivals and other church practices. Reformation does not mean revolution, throwing out the baby with the bath. The traditions of the church should be retained as long as they do not contradict Scripture, as long as they are in harmony with Scripture and strengthen the faith and life of the Christian people.

The Council of Trent (1545-1563) was the answer of the Roman Church to the Reformation, and its answer was wholesale condemnation. Martin Chemnitz, who stood third behind Martin Luther and Philip Melanchthon as champions of the Reformation, took up his pen to write a classic Lutheran response entitled, *Examination of the Council of Trent*, to explain how sixteenth century Lutherans understood the gospel of Jesus Christ, in distinction from the Roman bishops at the Council of Trent. He wrote with utter clarity on the *krinomenon* — meaning the critical point of difference concerning the article of justification through faith alone. This is not a fight over words among some squabbling theologians; it deals with what matters concerning the standing of every person before God.

Martin Chemnitz made the paradox of justification clear. I say "paradox" because it defies human reason and goes contrary to ordinary human expectation of what is just. It doesn't make sense that a sinner should get off scot-free without paying the right price. Sinners — that's all of us — are justified before God, prior to any change for the better in our sinful condition and always in spite of the fact that we can point to no inherent quality that puts us in a position to deserve the grace of God. The gospel of justification grants us forgiveness, creating a new relationship of acceptance before a righteous God, not because of any virtues we possess or good deeds we perform. It is truly liberating to know that there is simply nothing we must or can do to provide the basis for our standing justified before God.

Perhaps you remember the secular pop psychology of the 1970s called transactional analysis, in a self-help book written by Thomas Harris, *I'm OK – You're OK*. A good preacher will not miss the opportunity to ride piggy-back on what's current in literature and society. Thomas Harris said there are four states: 1) I'm not OK, You're OK; 2) I'm not OK, You're not OK; 3) I'm OK, You're not OK; 4) I'm OK, You're OK. Okay, what is it? What's the reality? Where do you stand, not merely horizontally in terms of yourself and other human beings (*coram hominibus*), but how do you stand where it really counts, before God (*coram deo*), vertically in the light of eternity? That's what we want to know. And the preacher with his wits about him, says, "I'm not OK and you're not OK"; but because of Christ, he is telling you, and that's the gospel truth, "You're OK." You are accepted, in spite of the fact that you are not OK. It's all about getting the prepositions straight, "not because of but in spite of." You're OK in spite of the fact you're not OK." It's all because of Christ. And that is what the doctrine of justification by faith is all about. Luther called it a "marvelous exchange."

Synergism is the heresy most antithetical to the doctrine of justification by faith. Synergism means that somehow we cooperate in our salvation. It makes salvation a fifty/fifty proposition. It means that we contribute something to our own salvation. Luther would say in his characteristic blunt language, synergism is the most damnable heresy ever invented, and it truly is. Why? Because it robs Christ of his glory; it nullifies Christ. It renders Christ unnecessary. And it makes way for boasting in ourselves, what we feel, what we have done, what we deserve. No, all our boasting is in the Lord, who has been made our righteousness (1 Cor. 1:30). Only Christ is the Victor over the powers of the demonic, sin, wrath, and damnation. Synergism, to the contrary, banks on the sweet message of positive thinking, that I'm OK, deep on the inside.

The sorry fact is that in the Lutheran tradition, especially in the tradition of Lutheran Pietism, synergism raised its ugly head to compromise the gospel of justification through faith alone. How so? When we say in the language common to our Reformation tradition that "faith alone justifies" and "faith alone is counted as our righteousness," the old demon of synergism threatens to take over the whole way of salvation. Our confessing fathers in the faith anticipated this possibility by saying that faith by which we are saved by grace is not in itself a human possibility. One of our Lutheran Confessions says, "Faith does not justify or save because it is a good work in itself." To be sure, faith is a good work, but it is the good work of the creative Spirit of God. Faith alone means Christ alone, for faith is the awareness worked by the Spirit that salvation is not from us, but for us. Humans in the state of sin do not have the free will to choose or not to choose the offer of God's grace. Faith is itself a free gift of the

Holy Spirit, a necessary gift without which we can not rejoice in the gift of salvation.

The Reformers did not deny that human beings have free will, but this freedom is limited to choice at the human level, preferring pies to cakes, or rooting for the Bears against the Lions. But this freedom does not avail before God, because our wills are in bondage to sin, death, and the power of the devil. So this is what happens to our human wills in the event of personal salvation: God makes unwilling persons will to do the will of Christ. Our wills in bondage need to be freed to will what God wills for us. All is of grace, that nothing shall be of works, not even the work of believing the true doctrines of the faith.

I need to add one caveat to all that I have said. The doctrine of justification by faith is not the gospel itself. No Lutheran preacher should imagine that a pulpit discourse on the Reformation doctrine of justification by faith gets him or her off the hook of preaching the gospel on Reformation Day. Giving a lecture on theology and preaching the gospel are two different things. Preaching the gospel promises the gift of forgiveness at the point of our greatest need — reconciliation with the God from whom we are estranged — fellowship with God our Creator through Christ our Redeemer — dealing with our common human predicament in its many dimensions — at enmity with God, alienation from others, and rejection of self.

A word to preachers: A preacher worth his or her salt will preach the gospel in such a way that every sermon answers the fundamental questions of human existence. There is no deeper question in human existence than how to get right with God. The gospel of justification through faith on account of Christ is the answer, not only for Lutheran sinners but for everyone. No sinner burdened by guilt and in the throes of despair can live a life fully to the hilt without the daily assurance of the forgiveness of sin. God accepts us just as we are, washes away our sin and guilt, in spite of the fact we are in ourselves woefully unacceptable by any stretch and unworthy of God's love.

WORLDWIDE ECUMENICAL RECEPTION OF THE DOCTRINE OF JUSTIFICATION BY FAITH

Now, how does this Reformation doctrine of justification by faith alone fare once we take it on the road in dialogue with other churches — Roman Catholic, Anglican, Methodist, and Reformed? In October, 1999, in Augsburg, Germany, the Roman Catholic Church and the Lutheran World Federation signed the "Joint Declaration on the Doctrine of Justification." At the time the good news was reported that they had "consigned to oblivion" the mutual condemnations of the sixteenth century. It must be admitted that some Lutherans and some Catholics received it as bad news. They couldn't believe what the Declaration states, "A consensus in basic truths of the doctrine of justification now exists between Lutherans and Catholics." And it goes on to say, "We give thanks to the Lord for this decisive step forward on the way to overcoming the division of the church."

As Lutherans we should bear one thing in mind. We should not require of our dialogue partners greater consensus on matters of doctrine than we have been able to achieve amongst ourselves. Remember the Helsinki fiasco. Member Lutheran churches of the Lutheran World Federation represented by their bishops and theologians met in Helsinki, Finland, in 1963.[33] First on their agenda was to draft a consensus statement on the doctrine of justification. If this doctrine is the one big thing for Lutherans, it would seem important for them not only to agree amongst themselves but also to present a united front to the rest of the Christian world. I call it a fiasco because they failed miserably. Germans and Scandinavians and Americans could not agree. First of all, confessional Lutherans who accepted the entire *Book of Concord* could not agree with those coming from the tradition of Lutheran Pietism. The old conflicts between Lutheran Orthodoxy and Lutheran Pietism were not resolved. At

---

33. *Proceedings of the Fourth Assembly of the LWF*, 1963 (Berlin: Lutherisches Verlagshaus, 1965), 57ff.

best they have agreed to disagree. Secondly, there were younger theologians, influenced by modern psychology, sociology, and existentialism who called for a new idiom and new language that modern people could understand. They issued a proclamation that asserted that "The Man of today no longer asks, 'How can I find a gracious God?' He suffers not from God's wrath, but from the impression of his absence; not from sin, but from the meaninglessness of his own existence; he asks not about a gracious God, but whether God really exists."

Ten years before this I read something Karl Barth wrote that gave me pause. He sounded a prophetic note that the Helsinki Lutherans completely ignored. He wrote, "Of all the superficial catchwords of our age, surely one of the most superficial is that, whereas 16th century man was occupied with the grace of God, modern man is much more radically concerned about God Himself and as such. As though there were such a thing as God Himself and as such, or any point in seeking Him! As though grace were a quality of God which we could set aside while we leisurely ask concerning His existence! As though the Christian community and Christian faith had any interest in the existence of God or nonexistent of this God Himself and as such."[34] At Helsinki Lutherans were mouthing exactly that superficial catchword, as though the question of the existence of God is a more radical existential question than that of the grace of God.

The good news is that the doctrine of justification by faith has gained new life in the modern ecumenical dialogues between Lutherans and other churches — Roman Catholic, the World Methodist Council, the World Communion of Reformed Churches, and it has also received positive affirmation from Baptist and Orthodox theologians.

The intention of the Joint Declaration is "to show that on the basis of their dialogue the subscribing Lutheran Churches

---

34. Karl Barth, *Church Dogmatics*, IV/1: 530.

and the Roman Catholic Church are now able to articulate a common understanding of our justification by God's grace through Christ." They agree, 1) "that all persons depend completely on the saving grace of God for their salvation"; 2) "that God forgives sin by grace and at the same time frees human beings from sin's enslaving power and imparts the gift of new life in Christ"; 3) "that sinners are justified by faith in the saving action of God in Christ"; 4) "that in baptism the Holy Spirit unites one with Christ, justifies, and truly renews the persons"; 5) "that persons are justified by faith in the gospel apart from works prescribed by the law"; 6) "that the faithful can only rely on the mercy and promises of God"; 7) "that good works — a Christian life lived in faith, hope, and love — follow justification and are its fruits." If you were a Roman Catholic and had a priest teaching and preaching the gospel according to those guidelines, you should count yourself so lucky. If you happen to be a Lutheran attending a Lutheran congregation today, you would be very fortunate to have a pastor teaching and preaching the gospel in light of those principles. That's my personal observation but I have no Gallup Poll stats to back me up.

But there are those, both among Roman Catholics and Lutherans, who have reacted to the "Joint Declaration" as fraudulent, as a fake consensus. Here is a statement from the Lutheran side, "We confessional Lutherans in the Lutheran Church Missouri Synod, the Wisconsin Evangelical Lutheran Synod, and the Evangelical Lutheran Synod do not agree with the 'Joint Declaration on the Doctrine of Justification.'" This is from churches that do not participate in any ecumenical dialogues, from churches that equate ecumenism with liberalism and believe they alone purely preach the gospel of salvation. The sad truth is that Lutherans and Catholics worldwide may now be closer together in doctrine, worship, and service than some Lutheran Churches are with each other. A number of Lutheran Synods do not permit their members to pray, worship, and commune with other Lutherans and they do not welcome those other Lutherans to participate in Holy Communion at their altars.

The fruit of the last fifty years of ecumenical dialogues is that those who call themselves evangelical, as I do, have become increasingly more catholic, and those who call themselves catholic have become increasingly more evangelical. George Weigel, a well-known Catholic author and commentator with impeccable Catholic credentials, has written a book entitled, *Evangelical Catholicism*, centered in the gospel of Jesus Christ. Robert Jenson and I, two cradle Lutherans, founded the Center for Catholic and Evangelical Theology 25 years ago. Our mantra is that Lutherans are evangelical catholics, as catholic as the Pope, but without the embellishments of Roman gold and elaborate gingerbread. We know that Luther never intended to start a new church named after him. He never became a Lutheran. He called for an evangelical renewal of the only church he knew, the church in which he was baptized, in which he was confirmed, and in which he was ordained. Luther said, "I ask that people make no reference to my name! Let them call themselves Christians, not Lutherans. St. Paul in I Corinthians 3 would not allow the Christians to call themselves Pauline or Petrine but Christians. What is Luther? After all, the teaching is not mine. Neither was I crucified for anyone. How should I — poor stinking maggot-fodder that I am — come to have people call the children of Christ by my wretched name? Not so, my dear friends. Let us abolish all party names and call ourselves Christians, after him whose teachings we hold."

All over the world many non-Lutheran Churches and Christians are joining Lutherans today in celebrating the Reformation. This makes clear that the Reformation does not belong to Lutherans alone. There are millions of Christians other than Lutherans who trace their spiritual DNA to 16th century Reformers other than Martin Luther — Ulrich Zwingli, John Calvin, Thomas Cranmer, John Knox, Thomas Müntzer, and there were reformers before them like John Wycliffe and Jan Hus. But more importantly Roman Catholics in many parts of the world are joining the celebrations, symbolized by the visit of Pope Francis to Lund, Sweden, urging reconciliation between

Catholics and Lutherans and acknowledging that the Reformation has been beneficial to the Roman Catholic Church as well.

Every doctrine has a history. Every generation re-reads Scripture in the context of its own experience and in its own time and place. In theology it's not true that there's nothing new under the sun. Reading the history of doctrine we learn that the *Nicene Creed* brings new ideas to the *Apostles' Creed* on the doctrine of the Trinity, and the *Creed of Chalcedon* brings new ideas on the person of Christ not contained in the *Nicene Creed*, and the *Athanasian Creed* adds new ideas to all of the previous Creeds. So also with the doctrine of justification. The Lutheran *Formula of Concord* added a more refined understanding of justification to what we read in the *Augsburg Confession*. And the beat goes on.

Finnish theologians at Helsinki University, headed by Tuomo Mannermaa, are advocating a new understanding of justification based on their re-reading of Luther's theology.[35] These Finnish theologians have been in ecumenical dialogue with Russian Orthodox theologians and in this context claim that for Luther faith is a real participation in Christ, that "in faith itself Christ is really and fully present." Righteousness is an attribute of God in Christ and this Christ in his divine person is really present in faith. Thus the Finns are critical of a purely forensic idea of justification, which they call a legal fiction. In the forensic model of justification we are regarded as though we are righteous but only in a nominal external sense, but not really, essentially and inwardly. In that case nothing would have changed. But in faith Christ is really present with his righteousness and that changes everything. Sinners are not the same anymore, because in faith Christ is truly present in his righteousness. Here lies the bridge to the Orthodox idea of salvation as deification or *theosis*.

---

35. See *Union with Christ. The New Finnish Interpretation of Luther*, edited by Carl E. Braaten and Robert W. Jenson (Grand Rapids, MI: Wm. B. Eerdmans Publishing Co., 1998).

Some German and American Lutheran theologians reject this new Finnish interpretation of Luther on the doctrine of justification. I do not bring this up to adjudicate who is right and who is wrong, since I am not a Luther-scholar *per se*, but to indicate that doctrines are not static things but develop through history. The truth is that if it were not for the Finnish intervention in the discussions leading to the final edition of the "Joint Declaration," it would never have seen the light of day. Creeds and confessions are living things in the stream of tradition. The old Greek philosopher, Heraclitus, was right, "You can never step into the same river twice."

JUSTIFICATION BY FAITH IS THE CHURCH'S DOCTRINE OF SALVATION

Justification by faith is the Church's doctrine of salvation. It does not belong to any one church, not to Lutheranism or to Protestantism as over against Orthodoxy and Catholicism. It belongs to the whole Church of Jesus Christ because it is the clear teaching of the Bible, especially in the theology of the apostle Paul. That's what the "Joint Declaration" affirms.

The dialogue between Lutherans and Catholics also reached the conclusion that it is not enough to reach a consensus on justification as a doctrine in and of itself. Why? Because justification without the church is a promise without the means to make it happen.[36] The church is God's chosen instrument to proclaim the justifying word of the gospel. Justification and church belong together in a mutual relationship. For Christ's sake God justifies sinners by grace through faith and makes them members of the church in baptism. Faith and baptism cannot occur without the church and its ministry of word and sacrament.

Justification and church are both works of the saving activity of the Triune God. A consensus reached between two

---

36. See *Church and Justification*, Lutheran-Roman Catholic Joint Commission (Published by The Lutheran World Federation, 1994).

separated churches on justification by faith cries out for taking further reconciling steps toward full visible unity. It is Christ who justifies us and as justified sinners we are the body of Christ — the church. According to the New Testament God's gift of justification and his election of the church are indissolubly linked. Jesus Christ is the only foundation of the church and he is the only way of salvation.

Thus, no church should have a strong soteriology — i.e., doctrine of salvation — as Lutherans tend to have, but then be weak on ecclesiology — the doctrine of the church — which is the common affliction of Protestantism, including some types of Lutheranism. But being weak does not mean being altogether dead. The chief concern of the Lutheran doctrine of the church is to stress its radical dependence on the gospel. In Luther's words, the church is the "creature of the gospel" (*creatura Evangelii*). The 62nd of Luther's 95 theses speaks of "the most holy gospel" as "the true treasure of the church." And Article 7 of the *Augsburg Confession* describes the church as "the assembly of all believers among whom the Gospel is preached in its purity and the holy sacraments are administered according to the Gospel." That is a good confession and pray God we continue to affirm it with passionate conviction.

However, the gospel proclaimed in Word and Sacrament doesn't just happen willy nilly. It happens by means of the special ministry of the church instituted by God. But here is where things began to fall apart in the history of Lutheranism. A deep contradiction in the Lutheran doctrine of the ministry has been exposed in the glaring light of ecumenical discussions, especially with Roman Catholics and Anglicans. Lutherans have historically held two contradictory concepts of ministry which can be traced to a basic inconsistency in Luther's thought.[37] To deal with this problem adequately would require more time

---

37. I have discussed this inconsistency in Luther's theology in my book, *The Apostolic Imperative* (Augsburg Publishing House, 1985), Chapter 8, "The Ecumenical Problem of Ordination and Succession."

than we have here. But this is the question. Is the pastoral office derived from below, from the congregation, from the laity, that is, from the priesthood of all believers as a matter of convenience and good order or is it derived from above, from a command of God, a holy office instituted by the Lord's will? When the young Luther was fighting against the priestly tyranny of Rome, he championed the first view. He said, what if a group of lay people found themselves on a desert island without a preacher, they could choose one of their own to preach and administer the sacraments. But when Luther was fighting against the radical reformation to the left, Thomas Müntzer and the Anabaptists, who got rid of the ordained pastoral ministry, Luther then put greater stress on the necessity of the office. Either the pastoral office was instituted by the will of Christ or it originated by the will of the people. If it came about by the will of the people, then it can be eliminated by the will of the people, and that is what the radical reformers did. No group of Lutherans ever went that far because they believed in the necessity of the gospel and the preaching of the Word and the administration of the Sacraments.

CONCLUSION

A meaningful 2017 celebration of the Reformation calls for renewed commitment to the ecumenical endeavors at home and abroad to heal the separations brought about by the Reformation. And we must celebrate not alone but with others who rejoice that the heart of the Reformation, the good news of God's justifying grace in the gospel, is alive and pulsating in the worldwide church, and that all significant partner churches affirm the doctrine of justification and not a single one has rejected it.

The unfinished business that is priority number one for the ecumenical movement is to reach sufficient agreement on ecclesial matters that still divide the churches. Neither Lutherans nor Anglicans, let alone Presbyterians or Methodists, have been able to meet the doctrinal requirements of the Roman Church for full communion and full visible unity. We have all attained far-reaching agreement on a host of doctrines — Trinity, Christology, justification by faith, baptism, eucharist, ministry, ordination. It bears repeating, the dogma of papal supremacy and infallibility remains the unbridgeable gap we cannot seem to overcome. And we cannot do it from our side. John Paul II indicated that the Pope needs to show that he is prepared to take seriously the legitimate criticisms of the papal office. He admitted that the ministry of the Bishop of Rome constitutes a difficulty for most other Christians. They harbor many painful memories. Then he adds, "To the extent we are responsible for these, I join my predecessor Paul VI in asking forgiveness." Paul VI confessed, "We are aware that the Pope is undoubtedly the greatest obstacle in the path of the *Oecumene*." The recent Popes have exhibited unremitting commitment to the ecumenical quest for church unity. They have welcomed to the Vatican the Bishops, Archbishops and Patriarchs from all other churches. They have joined in ecumenical celebrations with churches not in communion with the Roman Catholic Church.

Lutherans in dialogue have made it clear that they can envision a future of the church in which the Episcopate and the Petrine Office really function as signs and servants of the apostolic ministry and the evangelical mission of the church. However, at the same time they cannot accept the nineteenth century dogma in which the Pope declared himself infallible, nor are Lutherans today disposed to accept any heteronomous authorities, absolute principles, and inerrant documents. Reformation means freedom, "the freedom for which Christ has set us free" (Galatians 5:1).

The Pope is right when he said, "We all belong to Christ." We are all members of the body of Christ, and He has only one body. Edmund Schlink — once my professor of dogmatics at Heidelberg University and a veteran Lutheran ecumenical theologian whom I regard as my model — was one of several official representatives at the Second Vatican Council. He called for a "Copernican Revolution," such that all churches take Christ as their starting point, for He is the Sun around whom the churches revolve as planets and from whom we see the light that shines in the darkness of our world. It is by Christ and by Christ alone that all churches are to be judged and measured.

CHAPTER 6
ANGLICAN-LUTHERAN AGREEMENT ON THE GOSPEL

When I was asked by Bishop Ray Sutton to speak at this commemorative event celebrating the 500th anniversary of the 16th century Reformation, I accepted without any hesitation. But that was before I started thinking about what to say. Many voices are being heard lamenting what happened in 16th century Germany when the chubby monk from Wittenberg supposedly nailed his 95 Theses to the door of its Castle Church. What's there to celebrate? The mainline Protestant denominations — at least the major ones that trace their beginnings to the reforming principles of Martin Luther and Philip Melanchthon in Germany, Ulrich Zwingli and John Calvin in Switzerland, Thomas Cranmer and Richard Hooker in England, John Knox in Scotland — are the victims of three major trends, you might even call them tragedies, depending on your point of view. One, mainline Protestant denominations have drifted far from their founding confessions; two, they are conflicted by internal divisions and schisms; and three, they are shrinking, losing members by the millions, so much so, that some observers are speaking of the end of the Reformation and the end of Protestantism.

WHAT'S TO CELEBRATE?

Just to give you a brief sample of recent lamentations — Professor Ephraim Radner, an Anglican theologian and author of a pessimistic obituary of the global church in an ecumenical age, entitled *The End of the Church*, laments that the churches are in the mess they are because the Holy Spirit has abandoned the churches on account of their sinful separations. And because the Holy Spirit has taken leave of the churches, the gospel they profess to preach lacks credibility. And so, what's there to celebrate? How can we celebrate the divisions brought about by the Reformation and the membership decline we are witnessing today?

Robert Jenson, my long time friend, colleague and cohort in the church struggles in American Lutheranism, recently wrote an editorial in *Pro Ecclesia*, a theological journal we founded 25 years ago, "What's To Celebrate?" His answer is that we can hardly celebrate the separations caused by the Reformation. But there is something we can celebrate. We can celebrate what the Reformation contributed to the entire Church as a culture, appearing above all in its music, the hymns of Gerhard and the motets of Bach. What makes them so great is not that they are *about* faith; rather, they are in fact the happening of faith, the reality of faith itself, just as the Eucharist is not about Christ but just is the presence of Christ himself.

Sarah Hinlicky Wilson, editor of the *Lutheran Forum*, has offered her thoughts about the Reformation anniversary. She reminds us that Reformation Day used to be stirring occasions of celebration, culminating in lusty singing of "A Mighty Fortress." However, the ecumenical movement has singed our conscience with memories of the bad things triggered by the Reformation, the Lutheran acts of violence against Anabaptists, which the Lutheran World Federation apologized for in 2010, asking Mennonites for forgiveness. Lutherans have also apologized to Jews for the vicious words that Luther spoke against the Jews, words that helped to fuel the anti-Semitic attitudes of the German people during the Nazi period under Hitler, leading to the Holocaust.

There is much for which to repent and we cannot celebrate in a Christian way without repenting of the sins of our ancestors.

Nevertheless, Sarah Hinlicky Wilson writes, "We must celebrate. The proclamation of the gospel depends on it." Then she offers a fine summary of the gospel, which is sufficient cause for our rejoicing. She goes on with words that still resonate with many Evangelicals and perhaps even some Catholics: "Let us give thanks to God for giving us our teacher Martin Luther. Luther taught us a renewed love and attention to the Scriptures. He taught us that God comes down to us before we can rise up to Him.... He taught us the real presence of Christ in the act of baptism, in the words of absolution, and in the Supper.... He taught us to love the law of God that shows us how to live together, and he taught us to love even more the gospel that makes living together possible. He taught us to teach others with his Catechisms and translations. He taught us to sing." He taught us so many other things. Some of the best writing on Martin Luther in the 20th century has been by Catholic scholars — Joseph Lortz, Otto Pesch, Jared Wicks, and others.

IS THE REFORMATION OVER?

If the Reformation has come to an end, as some are saying, there would be no point to our celebration. You don't celebrate Grandmother's birthday once she's gone. Some Catholic voices rejoice to hear Protestant theologians announcing the end of the Reformation. When the Lutheran World Federation and the Pontifical Council for Promoting Christian Unity of the Roman Catholic Church signed the "Joint Declaration on the Doctrine of Justification," some concluded, "Aha! That means the Reformation protest is over. Good riddance!" There is supposedly nothing more to protest because the Reformers stated emphatically that the doctrine of justification by grace alone through faith alone on account of Christ alone is the chief point of difference, the article by which the church stands or falls. If the difference has been removed, doesn't that take the wind out of the sails of the protesting movement? Now, all we have to do is kill the fatted calf and welcome the prodigal son back home. It may take some time for Protestants to wake up and realize the new reality, but there is now no longer any obstacle in the way of reunifying the churches in the West, with their chief presiding officer at home in Rome.

Others see the turmoils and traumas occurring in denominational Protestantism as the convulsions of a dying corpse. Some Catholic hard-liners welcomed the news that the Vatican Congregation for the Doctrine of the Faith is opening the door for Anglicans dissatisfied with the Church of England to move toward full unity with Rome without making any major changes to their core beliefs, worship practices, and ministerial orders. Married priests may keep their wives but are prohibited from re-marrying. How many have done so, I do not know. Some oppose the ordination of female clergy; others oppose the ordination of homosexual priests; some oppose both. Schisms have occurred for similar reasons in mainline Protestant denominations. Shame on those Catholics guilty of *schadenfreude*, delighting in someone else's misfortune.

Now I would like to shift gears, and ask, "Are we really witnessing the last gasp of the Reformation, the waning of the confessional beliefs that inspired our fathers and mothers in the faith?" I would like to state my own conviction by quoting Mark Twain, "The reports of my death have been greatly exaggerated."

THE EVANGELICAL THRUST OF THE REFORMATION

Let me start with the evangelical thrust (*Ansatz*) of the Reformation. The Reformation did not invent a new Christianity. It did not preach a different gospel than what the apostles preached and what the apostle Paul enshrined in his Letters to the Romans and the Galatians. We are not here to celebrate the Reformation or Luther' theology or the *Augsburg Confession* or the *Book of*

Common Prayer or the *Thirty-Nine Articles*. We are here to celebrate the living voice of the gospel of Jesus Christ which was at the heart of the Reformers' witness and confession, and which had been largely muted in late medieval Catholicism. The question that was driving Luther crazy was, "How do I find a gracious God?" We may phrase the question differently today, like "How do I find ultimate meaning in my life?" The message of the Apostles and of the Reformers answered both of these questions in the same way. Jesus Christ is the revealing and redeeming act of God which makes people acceptable and righteous in his eyes. We celebrate the message of the gospel of God's love every time we celebrate the presence of Jesus Christ in Holy Communion. Is the Reformation over? Of course, as an event of past history it was over half a millennium ago. But what made it tick, the gospel of God in the person and ministry of Jesus Christ, lives on and will never perish from the earth. Kings and queens, emperors and dictators have tried to extinguish the gospel message of the Reformation and they have all failed.

The doctrine of justification by faith is not the gospel itself. The word "justification" is not the important thing. We refer to the same thing when we speak of the good news of God's forgiveness of sins on account of Jesus' death on the cross. Einar Billing, a Swedish scholar a generation ago, insisted that "anyone wishing to study Luther would indeed be in no peril of going astray were he to follow this simple rule: never believe you have a correct understanding of a thought of Luther before you have succeeded in reducing it to a corollary of the forgiveness of sins."[38] Of all the gifts the living God gives to us in our daily lives, surely the greatest is expressed by the words "forgiveness of sins." Those lucky ones who do no sin have no need of forgiveness. But you can forget about them; they don't exist. This gift of forgiveness touches us at the point of our greatest need. Our greatest human need is reconciliation with God from whom we are estranged.

---

38. Einar Billing, *Our Calling*, trans. Conrad Bergendoff, Facet Books (Philadelphia: Fortress Press, 1964), p. 4.

We need fellowship with God our Creator through Christ our Redeemer. Forgiveness of sins is God's act in Christ; he alone deals objectively and realistically with the human predicament in all its many dimensions.

The doctrine of justification has been a central concern of my life as a believer, as a preacher, and as a theologian. The doctrine frames the living voice of the gospel. Think of it as a signpost that points to the saving work of God in Jesus' sacrificial death on the cross and his victorious resurrection from the dead to a new mode of life with his Father in heaven. Preachers should proclaim the gospel in such a way that every sermon answers some fundamental questions of human existence. The struggle for love — is it worth it or will evil triumph? The quest for power — will it find the channels of peace or will we all be annihilated? The sense of guilt — is it only a feeling than an analyst can help us get rid of or is it a radically destructive condition that goes down to the roots of our being? The encounter with death — does it rob us of hope and threaten the meaning of life, or can we deny it by buying into a Platonic belief in the immortality of souls? What do we do with a conscience that demands more than we can give? Do we go on trying to satisfy it or do we mute its voice by denying its unconditional aspect? And what about hatred — so much in the air these days? Hatred of self, hatred of others, hatred of aliens? What kind of lies and delusions will we invent to mask what Kierkegaard called our "sickness unto death"?

And what about work? The majority of workers are not buoyed by a sense of high purpose. Rather, they are burdened by a sense of duty toward a job that easily degenerates into a menial task and monotonous drudgery. A large percentage of people are bored with their work, whether the farmer at the plow, the artisan in the shop, the parent doing chores, the scholar in the study, or the lawyer pleading a case in court. The Christian experience of receiving freely the absolving love of God in the forgiveness of sins can transform a job into a calling.

The prosaic present may be transformed into a sacred moment, when we receive the blessed assurance of unconditional love on account of Christ. We can praise and worship God in and through our work. We can give ourselves wholeheartedly to the work at hand, without expecting to derive our ultimate meaning and joy from the results of our labor. This is so because forgiveness frees us from grieving over the failures of our past and rescues us from dissipating our energies in worrying over the unknowable future. Christ is with us, Immanuel, come hell or high water! We can really take Jesus' words literally, "Therefore, do not be anxious about tomorrow, for tomorrow will be anxious for itself. Let the day's own trouble be sufficient for the day" (Matt. 6:34).

The thread that connects all the answers to these existential questions is the forgiveness of sins. No sinner burdened by guilt can live a life fully to the hilt without the daily assurance of the forgiveness of sins. God accepts us just as we are, washes away our sin and guilt, in spite of the fact we are in ourselves woefully unacceptable by any stretch and unworthy of God's love. The gospel of forgiveness of sins assures us that we can participate fully in the various structures of life without expecting that anything we do will deliver unambiguous good. The gospel of forgiveness offers us the motive and courage to act within the ambiguities of history and society, banking on the power, justice, and love of God as expressed in God's justification of the world in the life, death, and resurrection of Jesus Christ.

The "Joint Declaration" on justification signed by Lutherans and Catholics cleared the way for other significant developments. The Lutheran World Federation and the Pontifical Council for Promoting Christian Unity adopted a statement jointly commemorating the 500th anniversary of the beginning of the Reformation, entitled "From Conflict to Communion." Full Communion and full visible church unity are the explicit goal. Who can say that the last fifty years of ecumenical dialogue has accomplished nothing? This document begins by saying,

"We take as our guiding rule the doctrine of justification, which expresses the message of the gospel.... The true unity of the church can only exist as unity in the truth of the gospel of Jesus Christ.... Jesus Christ is the living center of our Christian faith.... The beginnings of the Reformation will be rightly remembered when Lutherans and Catholics hear together the gospel of Jesus Christ and allow themselves to be called anew into communion with the Lord."

ANGLICAN-LUTHERAN AGREEMENT ON JUSTIFICATION BY FAITH

But here we are at an Anglican Church. There is a lot of good news on this front as well. Lutherans and Anglicans have been in dialogue in Europe and Lutherans and Episcopalians have been in dialogue in the United States, starting with the acknowledgment that these two communions have never been in conflict. They have never condemned each others' doctrines. There has always been considerable proximity in matters of faith and worship. In the early years of the Reformation there were close ties between the reformers in Britain and on the Continent. The Lutheran influence left its mark on Cranmer's *Book of Common Prayer* and on the *Thirty-Nine Articles of Religion*. Both Anglican documents confess the doctrine of justification as a true formulation of the gospel of Jesus Christ. In the 20th century this was not forgotten. The Anglican-Lutheran Dialogue in Europe lifted up the doctrine of justification to a place of preeminent importance. It states, "It is in view of our common situation that the doctrine of justification takes on a fresh relevance.... The doctrine of justification is a fundamental part of our Anglican and Lutheran heritage.... Today we share a common understanding of its fundamental thrust.... We share a common understanding of God's justifying grace, i. e., that we are accounted righteous and are made righteous before God only by grace through faith because of the merits of our Lord and Savior Jesus Christ, and not on account of our works or merits.... The church is, indeed, the community of justified sinners."[39] The Lutheran-Episcopal Dialogue says the same thing and then adds, "The good news of salvation continues to comfort people of God and to establish them in the hope and promise of eternal life.... The gospel of justification continues to address the needs of human beings alienated from a holy and gracious God. Therefore, it is the task of the church to minister this gospel with vivid and fresh proclamation."[40]

Anglicans and Lutherans are now in full communion in Europe and the Episcopal Church in the United States and the Evangelical Lutheran Church in America are also in full communion. I have friends, retired Lutheran pastors, who tell me that now in their retirement they prefer to attend an Episcopal or Anglican Church because they can count on the liturgy, not knowing what they might get considering the worship wars and liturgical chaos in American Lutheranism.

RECEPTION OF THE REFORMATION BEYOND EUROPE AND AMERICA

The Reformation is not over. We are not celebrating or commemorating an event buried in the dust bins of past history. The effects of the Reformation have travelled beyond Europe and the United States. The younger Lutheran Churches in Africa, in particular, Ethiopia and Tanzania as well as Madagascar, where my parents were missionaries and where I grew up, are larger, more vibrant and faithful, and steadily growing compared to some of their parent missionary-sending churches in Europe and America which are declining at a rapid rate and increasingly compromised by a host of isms that have invaded their sanctuaries and institutions. A similar story can be told about

---

39. *Anglican-Lutheran Dialogue*. The Report of the European Commission (London: SPCK, Holy Trinity Church, 1983), pp. 8-9.
40. *The Report of the Lutheran-Episcopal Dialogue*, Second Series, 1976-1980 (Miniature Book, 1981), p. 23.

the worldwide Anglican Communion, which I must leave for others better informed to tell.

The Reformation is portable, it can travel, it's got legs, the legs of a pilgrim people who go wherever the church is being planted by the preaching of the gospel and the administration of the sacraments. I have a friend, a former graduate student whom I mentored at the Lutheran School of Theology at Chicago, whose name is Albert Garcia. He received a doctor's degree, taught theology for many years and is now retired. He was born and raised in Cuba as a Catholic, came to the United States and became an American citizen, and later became a Lutheran minister and theologian. He is the author and editor of two books that recount the spreading of the legacy of the Reformation among Hispanic speaking people. One book is entitled, *Wittenberg Meets the World, Reimagining the Reformation at the Margins*, and the other is, *Our 95 Theses. 500 Years After the Reformation*. Albert Garcia's aim is to correlate the message of the Reformation centered on the doctrine of justification with a post-colonial critique that addresses the history of oppression and the suffering and poverty of colonized peoples living at the margins of society. Garcia and his fellow Hispanic authors comprise one ecumenical voice from a wide variety of Christian traditions, from Catholic to Pentecostal and everything in between — Anglican, Lutheran, Methodist, Baptist, and Anabaptist. All of these authors acknowledge their evangelical roots in Luther, while at the same time voicing criticisms of the established churches for often failing to hear the cries of the people at the margins. Is the Reformation over? Not if we listen to these Hispanic theologians who minister and speak from the underside of society, moved by the word and the spirit of the 16th century Reformers — Luther, Calvin, Zwingli and others.

CONCLUSION

In conclusion I want to say that it is ecumenically salutary that Lutherans and Anglicans are together commemorating the

Reformation. Lutherans are known for their love affair with the gospel, for the pure preaching of the gospel so central in their self-understanding. Anglicans are known for their serious attention to the ordering of the ministry, namely, the threefold office of ministry, and in particular the historic episcopate, which was unintentionally lost to Lutherans in 16th century Germany. It's a loss that most Lutheran churches took steps to recover in the 20th century. It's also true that no church can live for long without the gospel of God's justifying grace in Jesus Christ. Sinners are incorporated into the community of faith called church through baptism by means of its sacramental ministry. Justification and the church are mutually implicative; they belong together,

CHAPTER 7
ANGLICAN-LUTHERAN AGREEMENT ON FULL COMMUNION

After his last trip to America in 1939, Dietrich Bonhoeffer, the German pastor and theologian imprisoned and martyred by Hitler's henchmen, wrote an essay entitled, "Protestantism without a Reformation."[41] It was a report of what he had personally observed in American Christianity. He wrote, "It has been given to Americans less than any other people in the world to achieve the visible unity of the church of God on earth. It has been given to Americans more than any other people in the world to manifest a pluralism of Christian beliefs and denominations."[42] Then Bonhoeffer further observed, "The rejection of Christology is characteristic of the whole of present-day American theology. Christianity basically amounts to religion and ethics in American theology. Consequently the person and work of Christ fall into the background and remain basically not understood in this theology."[43] He concluded his

---

41. Dietrich Bonhoeffer, "Protestantismus ohne Reformation," in *Gesammelte Schriften*, ed. Eberhard Bethge (Munich: Chr. Kaiser Verlag, 1958), 323-54.
42. *Ibid.*, p. 325.
43. *Ibid.*, p. 352, 354.

essay with a verdict and a challenge: "God has not given a reformation to American Christianity.... The decisive task today is to have a dialogue between American Protestantism without a reformation and the church of the reformation."[44]

Bonhoeffer's verdict rhymes with H. Richard Niebuhr's characterization of the preaching going on in Protestant Christianity in America. "A God without wrath brought people without sin into a kingdom without judgment through the ministrations of a Christ without a cross."[45]

If Bonhoeffer's observation is accurate, what are we doing here, celebrating the 500th anniversary of the Reformation in a nation whose churches have never experienced a reformation? The last fifty years of ecumenical dialogues between our separated churches is perhaps the closest we have come to a reformation, because in these dialogues we have challenged each other, shared each other's gifts, and realized the need for repentance face to face, all the while seeking the reform and renewal of the churches, to honor and obey the prayer of Jesus in John 17, "That they may all be one, that the world might believe."

ANGLICAN-LUTHERAN DIALOGUE ON THE MINISTRY

Full visible church unity has been the ultimate goal of the many ecumenical dialogues in the twentieth century. Both Lutherans and Anglicans became deeply engaged in dialogues with the Roman Catholic Church as well as with each other. While Lutheran Churches signed a far-reaching agreement with Roman Catholics on the doctrine of justification, Anglicans reached an equally far-reaching agreement with Roman Catholics on the doctrine of the church, on eucharist and ministry, on episcopacy and

---

44. *Ibid.*, pp. 353-54.

45. H. Richard Niebuhr, *The Kingdom of God in America* (New York: Harper & Brothers, 1937), p. 150.

papacy. Anglicans and Lutherans, along with Roman Catholics, believe that unity is of the essence of the church, and since the Church is visible, its unity must also be visible. But that is not yet the case, so the ecumenical dialogues will need to continue until the goal is reached.

The good news is that the goal of full visible communion involving mutual recognition of sacraments and ministry has been reached between the Nordic and Baltic Lutheran Churches and the Church of England in what is called the *Porvoo Agreement* as well as between the Evangelical Lutheran Church in America and the Episcopal Church USA in a statement of agreement, *Called to Common Mission*. Having read all the dialogues, I will offer a few generalizations before I get into the stickiest of issues having to do with episcopacy and apostolic succession. Lutherans tend to bear down hard on the doctrine of the gospel, on justification by faith, on the authority of Scripture, often seeming to assume that Anglicans were weak or somewhat indifferent on these matters. When the topics came up, Lutherans had their say, and what they insisted on, Anglicans were willing to affirm the Lutheran concerns. After all, at the time of the Reformation Anglicans and Lutherans shared a common confession and understanding of God's justifying grace, that is, that we are accounted righteous before God only for the merit of our Lord and Savior Jesus Christ, by faith, and not for our own works. For the last five hundred years Anglicans have never questioned the doctrine of justification, so all the dialogues between Anglicans and Lutherans have had clear sailing on soteriology, on the gospel and the way of salvation.

However, the discussions have not gone equally smoothly when it comes to ecclesiology, the doctrine of the church and its ministry, in particular the office of bishop in apostolic succession. Lutherans have been slow to get their act together. Many Lutherans in the Pietist tradition looked upon Anglicans as semi-Catholic. Having lost the office of bishop in the German Reformation, many Lutherans made a virtue out of a necessity, imagining it was a good thing to have a church without bishops. Lutherans of many stripes, not only Pietists, did not see it as a "tragic necessity," to use Jaroslav Pelikan's phrase. They saw it as necessary for the sake of breaking away from Rome. Reforming the church meant it was necessary to get rid of the whole kit and caboodle of bad bishops and their abuse of authority, but they did not see it as tragic, a rupture in the continuity of the church and a fracturing of its apostolicity. So Lutherans in America have had a lot of learning to do, playing catch up, having administered their churches with ordained pastors, superintendents or presidents, but allergic to calling their leaders bishops.

But not all Lutheran Churches have been opposed to the office of bishop. Episcopacy was preserved in unbroken historical succession at the time of the Reformation in Sweden and Finland. However, most Lutherans entered the dialogues with Anglicans and Episcopalians from a position of weakness, deeply divided on the doctrine of the ministry and the office of bishop. When the Evangelical Lutheran Church in America signed a watered down agreement with the Episcopal Church USA in 1999 that reached an accord on episcopacy, a thousand Lutheran congregations split away in protest, forming a loose association of congregations called, Lutheran Congregations in Mission for Christ.[46] They seem content to have a congregational polity, in which each local congregation is the church pure and simple, and no church reality exists beyond the local level. That is radical congregationalism. I don't agree with them. So I have been critical of those Lutherans who have opted out of the ecumenical movement or never joined it to begin with. Lutherans are not one big happy family. But neither are the Anglicans and the Episcopalians. So we have to limp along with fractures in both communions, Lutherans and Anglicans.

---

46. "Called to Common Mission" is a document that amends the "Concordat of Agreement." I use the term "water down" because the ELCA rejected the "Concordat," refusing to ordain bishops in apostolic succession. No one need be surprised if the ELCA is said to have bishops in name only. ELCA bishops are elected with term limits like USA senators – two six year terms.

CHURCH AND JUSTIFICATION BELONG TOGETHER

Among the books I have written, I have done one on the doctrine of justification and one on the church, which explains why I am pleased that Anglicans and Lutherans have been drawing closer together, even to the point of full communion. Each of them brings to the table a strong point, Lutherans with their emphasis on justification and Anglicans with their concentration on ecclesiology. Justification without the church is an empty word. The church without justification is an empty vessel. When I suggest that justification and church belong together, I am also saying that Anglicans and Lutherans have bonded together as never before at the points of their strength. Our faith encompasses justification and the church as works of the Triune God. The justification of sinners and the ministry of the church are not only linked with the Triune God but are founded on the sacrifice of the Christ and the sending of the Spirit. The chief concern of the Reformation was to highlight that the church lives on the basis of the gospel of God's justifying grace in Jesus Christ and is perpetually dependent on it, and on nothing else. Anglicans and Lutherans both teach that the church is a community of believers called and gathered together by the Holy Spirit through the proclamation of the gospel in sermon and sacrament.

Anglicans and Lutherans have often observed each other with a certain degree of mutual suspicion, partly because for the most part they have lived and ministered in different parts of the world, often speaking different languages and wearing different clerical vestments. Not seldom do Lutheran pastors show up in street clothes, mistakenly believing that it helps to connect with the people. Not without cause, Anglicans may harbor a concern whether the Lutheran understanding of justification as the be-all and end-all of what the gospel is about does not diminish appreciation of the church, and Lutherans often wonder whether the Anglican concern for the protocols of churchly practice does not obscure the gospel, which is the one thing needful. Whatever the case may be, both parties in dialogue now acknowledge that the New Testament knows of no opposition between gospel and church. The gospel of justification leads into ecclesiology and has no other home base.

STRUCTURES OF THE EMERGING APOSTOLIC CHURCH

The early church improvised answers to the question of how to keep the church apostolic in post-apostolic times. The question is still with us today, how can we be faithful to our apostolic origins when the passage of time makes us victims of forgetfulness? Initially the first Christians received their identity from the living witness of the apostles to the life, death, and resurrection of Jesus of Nazareth. Where this witness was absent, there could be no faith in Jesus as the Messiah of God and there could be no community gathered in his name, to praise and thank God for the promise of salvation.

We believe in the apostolic church. The apostolic nature of the church refers to the continuity of the church with Christ and the apostles from the past to the present. Apostolicity includes a variety of structures and institutions. It has been all too common for many people to think of apostolic succession primarily in terms of the historic episcopate. That is a narrowing of the concept, and let me explain why.

The first answer to the question how to keep the church in apostolic succession after the death of the apostles was to write things down to preserve their memories, and they did this by making a collection of the best of them. This is the canonical principle that refers to the New Testament Gospels and Epistles. The second answer was to preserve the earliest confessions having to do with baptism and that became the embryo of the Apostles' Creed. It is no little thing that Lutherans and Anglicans share the same canon and creed going back to the apostles, assuring that our churches remain apostolic now and into the future. The third is the cult, the pattern of worship. The core of the cult is sacramental, consisting of baptism, the Lord's Supper, and worship. Through these three media — canon, creed, and cult — the apostolic faith has been transmitted to our time, so that we can become contemporary with the first believers. Anglicans and Lutherans agree completely on these three mediations of the apostolic faith.

The rub comes when we consider the fourth medium of apostolic faith — a special ordained ministry to Word and Sacrament, grounded and legitimated in the teaching of the apostles. New Testament scholars speak of "early catholicism" in the Pastoral Epistles (e.g., I & II Timothy). In this development we have the beginnings of the ordained ministry as we know it now. The church could not get along with purely charismatic ministries. A process of institutionalization was deemed necessary for the sake of good order, to care for such down-to-earth things as canon, creed, and cult. They don't take care of themselves. Anglicans and Lutherans in dialogue agree that a special ordained ministry in the church began in the early church and is needed as much today as ever. Basically, it is a matter of leadership in the church for the sake of continuity with the witness of the apostles to Jesus Christ. At the same time both churches agree that a special ordained ministry does not take away from the ministry of every baptized Christian. We call this the universal priesthood of all believers. Yet, a special ministry is needed to lead the church into fruitful and faithful continuity with the church's apostolic foundation, with Christ as its chief cornerstone. The ordained minister is called to be a leader of the community, not as a master, ruler, or boss, but simply as a servant performing functions that flow from the fullness of the gospel. The special ordained ministry is radically subordinate to the cause of Jesus and the gospel the apostles proclaimed.

Sad to say, church history tells us that at times duly called and ordained ministers of the church have become enemies of the gospel and serve the interest of the counter-Christ. It happened in the early church and it is happening today. Heresy or apostasy arises when a church leader seriously distorts or denies the canonical and creedal norms which the ancient church fathers developed to retain its identity and continuity with the apostolic witness of Jesus Christ. Do we have notoriously bad pastors and priests in the churches today, Anglican, Lutheran, Methodist, or Roman Catholic? It should not be too surprising. The apostle Paul warned that there would be false prophets — hirelings — who would invade the congregations to preach and teach an alien gospel and false doctrine. *The Apology of the Augsburg Confession* states: "We should forsake wicked teachers because they no longer function in the place of Christ, but are anti-Christs."[47]

Anglicans have been much more clear than Lutherans on the theology of the ordained ministry. Lutherans have spoken with forked tongue on the doctrine of the ministry. The low church tradition holds what is called the transference theory. The rights and powers that belong to all believers are delegated to one person who performs certain functions. For the low church tradition that prevailed in Pietism ordination is deemed to be simply a ceremony of installation and ratification of a congregational call. The Constitution of one Lutheran Church declares that "the status of the clergy differs from that of the laity only as to function."[48]

The high church view asserts that the ordained ministry is divinely instituted; it possesses sacramental character, by which the Holy Spirit bestows a certain charism by means of prayer and the laying on of hands, effecting a transmission of gifts by ministers already in office. Prominent theologians can be quoted on either side of this ambivalence in the Lutheran tradition. Anglicans have a right to be suspicious of their Lutheran partners in dialogue, noticing that Lutherans have never agreed

---

47. Article 28, *The Apology*.
48. *The Constitution and Bylaws of the American Lutheran Church*, 6, 32-33.

among themselves on the matter of ministry. The upshot is that Lutherans who do not agree with the high church view simply withdraw from the ecumenical agreements and form a sectarian association of their own.

THE HISTORIC EPISCOPATE

Given the Lutheran ambiguity on the doctrine of the ordained ministry, there is little wonder that when it comes to the threefold office of the ministry — bishop, priest, and deacon — maintained by Anglicans since the time of the Reformation, Lutherans have had a struggle, nationally and internationally, to find common ground. Anglicans have had their own struggle with respect to the historic episcopate. The Anglo-Catholicism of the 19th century Tractarian movement offered serious arguments that the historic episcopate is not optional. Rather, it is of the essence (*esse*) of the church, and if so, churches without the historic episcopate are to that extent ecclesiologically defective. However, the Anglicans and Episcopalians that Lutherans have met in dialogue have not taken that view. They have never "unchurched" non-episcopal churches, but hold instead that the historic episcopate is for the well-being (*bene esse*) of the church, contributing to the fullness of the church (*plene esse*).

By and large Lutherans in dialogue have reached an agreement with their Anglican counterparts on the historic episcopate, not because they thought their churches were deficient without it, but because they were free to do so. There was no *nihil obstat* in their confessional writings. In fact, to the contrary, they could point out that the Lutheran Reformers were in favor of the office of bishop, stating that "the power of bishops is a power or command of God to preach the Gospel, to remit or retain sins, and to administer sacraments."[49] All Scandinavian Lutherans retained the office and title of bishop, and in the 20th century

---

49. *Anglican-Roman Catholic International Commission, The Final Report* (Windsor, 1981), 97.

more and more Lutheran churches adopted the title of bishop for their district presidents. And where Lutheran missionaries from Scandinavia planted new churches in Africa, as in Tanzania and Ethiopia, they installed the historic episcopacy. I can state with a high degree of confidence as a Lutheran theologian that it is entirely acceptable to acknowledge that the historical development of an episcopate in apostolic succession is something that has taken place with the help of the Holy Spirit and that it is not simply of human design. As Anglicans and Lutherans look beyond themselves, they will seek to promote the unity of all churches that claim to hold the faith of the one, holy, catholic, and apostolic church.

LUTHERANS AND ANGLICANS IN DIALOGUE WITH ROMAN CATHOLICS

While Lutherans and Anglicans have been in dialogue with each other reaching agreement on the doctrine of the gospel and the ministry of the church, they have at the same time been engaged in dialogue with Roman Catholics. When Lutherans and Catholics signed a "Joint Declaration on the Doctrine of Justification," they were able to conclude: "A fundamental consensus on the gospel is necessary to give credibility to our previous agreed statements on baptism, on the Eucharist, and on forms of church authority. We believe we have reached such a consensus."

So where does the shoe pinch? What stands between the two churches, Lutheran and Catholic, on which there is yet no consensus? The big elephant in the room is not the papacy as such, but rather the 19th century dogma of papal jurisdiction and infallibility which has propped up its claim to universal authority. And yet Lutherans and Catholics in dialogue have tackled every aspect of the papal office. But so have Anglicans and Catholics done so. And as far as I can tell, they have not become more affirmative of the papal office in its present configuration than have Lutherans. The *Final Report of the Anglican-Roman Catholic International Commission* (1981) has some interesting things to say. Like Lutherans the Anglicans in this dialogue say that they find grave difficulty in the affirmation that the pope can be infallible in his teaching. They cite as examples the Marian dogmas, expressing serious doubt that they are essential to the faith of believers. Lutherans would agree with that. The First Vatican Council affirmed that the ministry and authority of the bishop of Rome is necessary to the unity of the whole church. The Council used the language of "divine right" of the successors of Peter. Anglicans, however, cannot accept that churches not in communion with the bishop of Rome are less than fully a church. Anglicans in this *Report* express reservations about the Pope's universal jurisdiction because it has all too frequently exercised power in illegitimate ways.

Vatican II took pains to replace the juridical outlook of the 19th century with a more pastoral understanding of the Pope's authority in the church. Pope Francis is living proof that it can make a difference in how the Pope's ministry is perceived by non-Catholic churches and Christians. At the bottom line Anglicans like many Lutherans do not object to the universal primacy of the Roman bishop, as the first among equals, but rather they object to the abuses of the papal power, as well as the inflated dogmatic claim of infallibility buttressing his authority. The Anglicans state: "We agree that the term 'infallibility' is applicable unconditionally only to God, and that to use it of a human being, even in highly restricted circumstances, can produce many misunderstandings. That is why in stating our belief in the preservation of the Church from error we have avoided using the term. We also recognize that the ascription to the bishop of Rome of infallibility under certain conditions has tended to lend exaggerated importance to all his statements."

The Lutheran Confessions demonized the Papal office by calling Pope Leo the "Anti-Christ." No Lutheran with any conscience would even think of calling any of the modern Popes the anti-Christ. Regrettably some Lutherans who claim to be super-orthodox still do. Webster's Dictionary has a word for such — troglodytes. Pope John II exhibited unremitting commitment to the ecumenical quest for church unity. He took pilgrimages to various churches on different continents. He mentions in particular his visit to the headquarters of the World Council of Churches, his ecumenical meetings with the primate of the Anglican Communion at Canterbury Cathedral, with the Ecumenical Patriarch Dimitrios I, and with Lutheran bishops and archbishops of the Scandinavian and Nordic countries. He joined in ecumenical celebrations with churches not in communion with the Roman Catholic Church.

The Pope expresses appreciation that the question of papal primacy has been seriously discussed in the ecumenical dialogues with Anglicans, Lutherans, and the Orthodox. However, with their best efforts we still have no consensus to motivate the drive toward full communion and visible church unity. The papacy is itself the chief obstacle and none of the dialogues has succeeded in removing it. Lutherans and Anglicans have made it clear that they can envision a future of the church in which the episcopate and the Petrine office really function as signs and servants of the apostolic ministry and mission of the church.

In the Middle Ages there was an abbot of a monastery in Southern Italy by the name of Joachim of Floris. He had a prophetic dream that envisioned a future transformation of the hierarchical church into a spiritual community and a conversion of the authoritarian model of papal power into the service of an angelic pope, a *papa angelica*, who would represent freedom in the life of the Spirit.

I am going to end this talk by suggesting that what we need now is not an angelic pope but an evangelical pope who will lead the divided churches on the path to reconciliation. Papal primacy need not be a barrier to reconciliation that embraces diversity, honoring various church traditions of piety and worship as gifts of the Spirit — from Anglican to Pentecostal and the rest of us in between. A reformed and restructured papacy can be accepted by non-Roman churches as a special function of the universal church serving the ministry of the gospel throughout the world. This is what the Reformers wanted from the beginning, episcopal and papal offices that would serve the gospel and not lord it over the people like autocratic princes. When God Almighty brings that to pass, we will have a lot to celebrate, not only the birthday of the Reformation that led to the division of the churches but the reunion of the divided churches to make fully visible the one, holy, catholic and apostolic church on earth, in which we all claim membership.

Pg 21 - Gospel

Made in the USA
Monee, IL
16 April 2024